METAPHYSICAL DIVINE WISDOM

on Increasing Prayer with Faith for an Abundant Life

A Practical Motivational Guide to Spirituality Series

KEVIN HUNTER

WARRIOR
OF LIGHT
PRESS

Warrior of Light Press
www.kevin-hunter.com

First Edition: July 2019
Printed in the United States of America

All rights reserved. Copyright © 2019
ISBN-13: 978-1733196246

3. Mind and Body. 2. Spirituality. 1. Title

DEDICATION

For you on your soul's spiritual journey.

METAPHYSICAL DIVINE WISDOM
BOOK SERIES

On Psychic Spirit Team Heaven Communication
On Soul Consciousness and Purpose
On Increasing Prayer with Faith for an Abundant Life
On Balancing the Mind, Body, and Soul
On Manifesting Fearless Assertive Confidence
On Universal, Physical, Spiritual and Soul Love

♥

Contents

AUTHOR NOTE

The *Metaphysical Divine Wisdom* books are a series of spiritually based books that focus on different areas of one's life. Like many of my spiritual related metaphysical books, this one is also infused with practical messages and spirit guidance that my Spirit team has taught and shared with me revolving around many different topics. The main goal is to fine-tune your body, mind, and soul. Like all souls, you are a Divine communicator capable of receiving messages and guidance from Heaven.

My personal Spirit team council makes up God and the Holy Spirit, as well as a team of guides, angels, and sometimes Archangels and Saints. I am merely the liaison or messenger in delivering and interpreting the intentions of what they wish to communicate. My team comprises some hard truth telling Wise Ones from the Other Side, including Saint Nathaniel, who can be brutal in his direct forcefulness. He cuts right to the heart of humanity without apology. I have learned quite a bit from him while adopting his ideology, which is Heaven's philosophy as a whole. I wouldn't preach Divine Guidance that God doesn't whisper into my Clairaudient ear first.

If I use the word "He" when pertaining to God, this does not mean that I am advocating that he is a male. Simply replace the word, "He" with one you are comfortable using to identify God for you to be. If the word, "God" makes you uncomfortable, then substitute it with one you're more familiar with like Universe, Spirit, the Light, or any other comparable word. This goes for any gender I use as examples. When I say, "spirit team", I am referring to a team of 'Guides and Angels'.

One of the purposes of my work is to empower, enlighten, as well as entertain. It's also to help you improve yourself, your soul, your life and humanity by default. If anything, I am preaching to myself, because God knows that I can use a refresher course once in a while. It does not matter if you are a beginner or well versed in the subject matter. There may be something that reminds you of something you already know or something that you were unaware of. We all have much to share with one another, as we are all one in the end.

~ Kevin Hunter

METAPHYSICAL DIVINE WISDOM

ON INCREASING PRAYER WITH FAITH FOR AN ABUNDANT LIFE

CHAPTER ONE

The Power of Prayer

They say ask and you shall receive. I've been a strong advocate for prayer and asking for Divine help since childhood. It's been one of my longtime goals to devote a book that primarily points to having faith and asking for Divine heavenly assistance because of the endless miracles I've witnessed come about whenever I'd pray as opposed to not praying. My mother taught me to pray before I was five years old, but she wasn't religious or particularly a big believer. It was just standard practice by many families when I was growing up. Still her coming into my room every night as a young child before bed to pray was enough for me to take that and run with it more than anyone anticipated.

I was a strong promoter for prayer by the time I was seven years old. This was long after my mother stopped the nightly prayer ritual. I continued with it because I was seeing positive results come out of it, especially as I grew older into the teenage and young adult years. A great deal of my psychic and mediumship lessons was during my childhood years. My teachers were my Spirit team council of guides that have been around me since childhood as well too. I was seeing and hearing spirit naturally from a young age that it was enough for me to be convinced of a life beyond this one. I'm someone that is naturally skeptical and analytical before anything else, but it has been my repetitive testing of my Spirit team that has kept my faith. A great deal of what I discuss in many of my spiritual works are things that I was taught by them. This is why sometimes it might seem familiar and other times it might feel as if I've gone rogue from what people expect in the spiritual related genre.

One of the many things I've learned from my Spirit team was that the entire time I was talking to them that it was also considered prayer. Whether you are having a conversation with them, making an affirmation or statement, then you are essentially praying. When I have a problem I immediately go directly to God and my Spirit team to discuss it. If I'd need an answer that wasn't forthcoming, then I'd continuously ask them, "You've got to give me something on this. Anything."

Within a few days the answer would come in that was pleasing enough for my ego to drop it for awhile. It gave me the comfort and peace of mind that would remind me to relax and understand that things are moving towards the wanted desire. When it's time for what I want to surface, then it will take place on Divine timing. Eventually I'd see it surface and I'd quickly be grateful and blessed.

I'd say, "Okay, I'm sorry I'll never doubt again."

That of course is a lie. Because once my ego rises again on something I want that isn't happening fast enough, I'd repeat the cycle with them. I'm certainly not exempt from watching my ego rise. The difference is that I'm hyper cognizant and aware I've moved into that space. If the ego is strong enough I'll rebel and say, "I don't care right now. I need to stomp around and get this out of me."

As my soul's consciousness evolved over the years, the tantrums grew less as I learned to be more patient than I normally was. The majority of the time I've learned with maturity to bring it down quickly, then of course again I'm apologizing for my behavior. They're unfazed by it and understand that I'm wrestling with the dreadful dark human ego. I'll pray to help relax and contain it, then help me get re-centered again into warrior mode. As I've grown older it's become easier to master.

Friends and family could be having an issue and I'd interrupt to say, "I'm going to stop you right there. Have you prayed for help with this?"

Ah-okay, you're welcome.

Sometimes I'll receive silence for a beat, then the other party meekly says, "Well no because...".

I interrupt, "Okay well do you want help or not? Look, nothing else you're doing is working right now, so what do you have to lose by asking for heavenly help in prayer?"

I've had some ask, "How do I pray? I don't know how."

They've never done it before or might not have grown up in a house that believed in prayer or considered it, so therefore they weren't taught to know how easy it is. I've had those same people come back to me weeks later, "You're not going to believe this, I finally got a breakthrough! The praying actually worked! I can't believe it. You were right."

Some never believed in prayer or bothered with it much because they assumed it was something that only the serious religious do. Prayer is not a special act that belongs to any particular group. Prayer is allowed to do by anyone at anytime regardless if you are a believer or not. You might ask God or your Spirit team for something in prayer verbally, but in your heart they know what you really want. It is what is in your heart that Spirit reads.

You might ask for something less than what you desire, because you fear asking for too much. You desire that home of your dreams in a certain area, but you ask for something smaller because you're afraid to go big. With that scenario some have become surprised when they asked for one thing, but received something even better. When I started praying for help on certain things I desired, I'd watch one year go by, then another, and another. I didn't give up hope or stop praying. Years from the point when I started praying, I finally got that breakthrough and that long running desire I wanted was granted.

There is a reason God delays certain blessings. He may have something much bigger than you had in mind and that takes longer to make happen. Do you want something menial that will be disappointing in the end right away? Or do you want to wait a bit longer for the big gold that ends up lasting? I'll be patient and wait a bit longer.

I've had someone tell me he was having constant issues at work. I asked him, "Have you prayed for help with that?"

He asked, "You can pray for something like that?"

I said, "You can pray for anything you like. There's no requests that are exempt from being asked for."

He asked, "What if it's not something God approves of or it's something greedy?"

I said, "Then He won't give it to you."

One of the other things I've been taught from my guides is that while prayers help for other people to an extent, the daily prayers coming directly from the person in trouble is a hundred times more effective. When you're praying for other people you're driving at 25 mph, but the person that prays daily for their own stuff increases that speed to 60 mph. This is to breakdown the discord in understandable terms. If you're praying for someone that isn't a believer or isn't bothering to pray, then the effectiveness is only a mild improvement that could increase if the other person does it too. The exceptions would be someone that is incapable of praying such as if they are in a coma.

Sometimes heavenly assistance is not forthcoming for a variety of reasons. It could be you are being guided to take action steps that will help move you out of the stagnancy you're in, but you're either not picking up on this guidance, or you have fear about making this move because it might feel that it's moving you out of your comfort zone and into a negative repercussion. God nor any high vibrational spirit being in Heaven will guide you into a disaster. What might seem like a scary move could be the one that ends up propelling you upwards into the sphere of Divinity.

This doesn't mean that God and your Spirit team sit back and act like Genie's in a bottle waiting to grant your wishes. If one is only praying for abundance and gifts, but isn't doing the soul growth work, then this will play a part in whether or not blessings will come.

Playing on your phone and surfing the Internet all day blocks divinely guided psychic messages. It's a distraction that pulls you away from heavenly communication that is attempting to filter in. This isn't said with the intention of instilling guilt feelings for being on your phone. This is about counter balancing some of those moments by devoting at least a few minutes to ten minutes a day to communicate in prayer. How often have you reached for your phone out of boredom instead of taking a few minutes to give God some of your time?

Praying persistently and daily isn't just praying for blessings, money, love, or a new job. This is also about offering gratitude and humility. You express your appreciation for the things that are going well in your life. It also helps in establishing a stronger relationship with God and your Spirit team. In order for any relationship to thrive and grow stronger you have to show up. You have to put in the work and communicate with one another. The same goes for God and your heavenly guardians. You don't want to turn into an entitled soul only going to Spirit with a list of daily demands.

Imagine that you have kids if you don't, and every time they walk in the door they're only asking you for things. They never talk to you unless they need something from you. You would get annoyed pretty fast that that's all they see you as and that they have no interest in spending time with you at all. This is to offer some perspective of God as the parent and you as the child. He nor heavenly beings mind it when you ask for blessings or help with things that give you comfort such as security. They'd also like it more if you were interested in spending time with them because you want a relationship, and not because you want them to keep giving you presents and opening doors to abundance.

You can put in requests with Heaven for blessings and desires, but also offer gratitude, be grateful, and see how you can positively be of service to them. Blessings won't automatically land on your lap with the snap of the finger. They may be planting action steps into your consciousness for you to take that should be adhered to. When you're receiving nudges, signs, and symbols of the same thing repeatedly, then don't ignore that. The Devil, Darkness, and your lower self's ego will do its best to sway you from taking action through procrastination and negative thoughts and words. I've learned that the hard way during my days of human adolescence.

The Devil's goal is to wear people out, which he can do by attacking your mind. Those negative thoughts that talk you out of good things are the Darkness getting in there to prevent you from moving forward. God and the Light want to see you prosper, evolve, and thrive on all levels. While the Devil and Darkness prefer the opposite where they help you to create your own self-sabotage and downfall.

The Darkness will infect your mind with lies. This soon affects your thoughts and then your emotions. The dark energy wants people independent from God's will. That's why he grows angry when someone defies that and doesn't fall for his deceit, because then he knows he lost another soul to the Light, which he can't stand. The way to anger the Darkness is to stand strong in the Light.

The Darkness can work through other people to attempt to stall you from moving forward. It's the same way the Light can work through people. I've definitely spent this lifetime having the enemy attempt to stall me by using other people as pawns, which is super easy to do. Luckily, the Light has countered that by then working through other people to undo whatever the Darkness just tried to do. This is the moment you feel Divine empowerment.

Some look at empowerment as a negative word. Empowerment is not about gaining fame or financial success. Empowerment here is more about feeling soul and spirit empowerment because God is working through you from the inside and out. The side effect would be success on some level, but that's not the goal. Empowerment is waking up each day with a bright new optimistic outlook. It's a sign the angels are working on you and your consciousness is receiving that in the right spirit. I know that feeling well as it seems to naturally move within me regularly. When I've had those lower moments in my past such as a relationship break up or any disappointment, then deep down I know there is that warrior soul strength that is lit by the Divine. It always eventually rises up back within me prompting me to stand tall preparing to aim, seize, and fire! The empowering moments continue to rise and rise again.

CHAPTER TWO

Be Vigilant with
Prayer and Affirmations

So many struggling to make ends meet, struggling to get by, struggling uphill period. This isn't unusual as humankind has infinitely struggled throughout Earth's history to achieve peace and happiness. That's one thing that most everyone can agree on. The goal is the same for all and that is to be happy. Even the permanent miserable grumps deep down in their soul essence long for that joyful content feeling. It makes you feel good and blasts away any moody irritable unhappiness.

As you read this now, I surround you with the Light of the Holy Spirit as well as angels who are of

100% pure uplifting love and to help in raising your vibration and to assist you along your life's path and purpose.

When in doubt, ask for help from above, even if you don't see evidence of movement. If your faith wavers due to lack of evidence, then ask to have your faith boosted. Miracles happen daily as Guides and Angels in Heaven work tirelessly guiding every soul on the planet to make life a little more pleasant. That's seven billion souls living an Earthly life with at least one guide and one angel per person. That's at least 14 billion spirit beings guiding every human soul on the planet. They can only do so much. Their job is to guide you, not hand you everything the second you ask for it. They are also dealing with the free will choice of human beings. Most people are not that in tune to the guidance and messages coming through from above, nor do they understand how to recognize it, yet each and every soul has the strong capacity for receiving incredible psychic hits.

It's not like Heaven can drop a bucket of cash on everybody's doorstep as much as many people would rather enjoy that. What would everyone learn if that were the case? Those who are well to do financially are also not exempt from troubles I can assure you. If something isn't forthcoming, then there are reasons beyond what you cannot comprehend or understand at the time. There are also circumstances and experiences that you need to be enlightened about on your own.

Sometimes heavenly assistance is not

forthcoming for a variety of reasons. It could be that you are being guided to take action steps that will help move you out of the stagnancy you're in, but you're either not picking up on this guidance, or you have fear surrounding this move since it might feel like it's moving you out of your comfort zone. You fear a negative repercussion, but no high vibrational spirit being in Heaven will guide you into a disaster. What might seem like a scary move could be the one that ends up moving you upwards.

I have forever believed in the power of prayer. This is not because it's taught in some circles to do. This is because I have witnessed miraculous intervention and changes in my own life as well as for others only after I prayed. When I did nothing, then nothing changed. When I asked for assistance or prayed, then I noticed positive changes come about. I wouldn't continue with anything unless I knew it worked. This is one of the many reasons I have been a lifelong advocate of prayer.

Sometimes Divine intervention happens immediately, while other times the assistance isn't forthcoming right away, but with those cases I have noticed it eventually comes to fruition at some point. I have incorporated daily prayer throughout the course of my entire life because it works.

Many are usually surprised over the humor that pops in and out at times while talking to Heaven. That's because Heaven is not some stern, harsh, cold place. It's filled with uplifting love, peace, and joy. Those are qualities that all beings in Heaven exude. They are bathed in those energies, which equates to also having immense humor. You can then likely gather that this is how they view circumstances in the practical based Earthly world. They see most of what goes on in a humor filled light rather than the tragic offended manner that many on Earth view circumstances around them in.

Some atheists or non-believers do not accept prayer as anything that works, but they're also unaware that they are praying without realizing it. I've heard of cases where a non-believer takes time out each day to sit with their thoughts. In that instance, they are communicating with God whether they believe they are or not. You are a piece of God. Every atom and cell that exists in all dimensions are Him.

You can use prayer to boost your faith, reduce fear, and give you crystal clear psychic perception. Prayers are much like affirmations in that it is the intention behind the words that have weight. The stronger your intention within your prayers, then the brighter the light around it is.

Heaven sees affirmations and prayer as lights being shot upward into the Universe. These lights are of varying shades. Some prayers have a brighter and stronger light around them, while other prayers appear dimly lit if it's a prayer or affirmation that has ego-based property energy within it that benefits no one except the ego. Other times the dimly lit prayers can be requests that are not considered urgent. It could be you really want that brand-new tech gadget that the store just received, whereas a brighter lit prayer would be coming from someone who is in immediate physical danger.

Children's prayers tend to have some of the brightest lights around them. Part of that has to do with the fact that most Children have not become jaded and believe in a higher power, whereas an adult might have some doubt energy within their prayer, which actually darkens the light being shot into the air. Asking for a boost in faith strengthens this light within the prayer.

During the early childhood days when my mother was praying with me, one of the things that stood out was there was no judgment or negativity associated with these prayers at all. She is an incarnated angel, so those prayers were bathed in 100% compassion for all people. My mother's faith eventually waned over the years and my father struggled to have some resemblance of faith. It was ironic that in an extended family that I had the most faith that would only grow stronger as I moved into adulthood. Part of this was due to the fact that I could hear my Spirit team, so I knew there was something bigger than the physical plane that existed. I mainly grew up in a home of atheists and agnostics, but as I grew more vocal with my teachings many of the family members slowly awakened their skepticism. The point of that is I wasn't influenced by anyone around me growing up when it came to my spiritual beliefs. It was Heaven that heavily influenced me.

Many people sometimes feel as if they're not loved by the Divine, or that they're being ignored, neither of which are true. All are loved and no one is ignored. When it feels that way, then that has to do with your feelings, which ebb and flow. Feelings are not incessantly accurate when it's a reaction generated by the ego. The best way to feel loved by the Divine varies from one person to the next, but you can start by increasing your faith, having regular prayer and conversations with the Divine, even if it feels like you're talking to no one. You are heard and eventually you start noticing the signs that you're not alone and that you are loved. In the physical world, the ego requires physical concrete material evidence of that love, but the love is felt from within like a great big warm hug.

I find all forms of prayer have worked and have been equally successful for me. This is regardless of hands clasped together, in meditation, in writing, or while in motion. There hasn't been one method that works better than the others. This is because it doesn't matter how you do it, but that you do it. The most immediate way of receiving answers in a prayer is while in a calm state of mind, which means that sometimes the response will come about long after the prayer was executed.

Have the intention that you will clearly hear, see, feel, and know the messages and guidance Heaven wishes to relay to you. Visualize crystal clear bright white light shining onto your soul in order to awaken it from slumber. Imagine the white light blasting away any and all of the toxic dark debris that may have accumulated on or around you.

The psychic clair senses within all souls are nothing unusual, because it is through those senses that the spirit and soul communicate with one another back home on the Other Side. Soul mates or couples that are super tight on Earth have a telepathic communication between one another where they are able to sense what the other is going through or thinking. Some people have joked that they wished they could read someone's mind. Well, back home in Heaven that is how others communicate with each other. There are no lies created, because everyone already knows the truth.

You may also call upon a specific Archangel to assist in opening up your various psychic clair channels. Below are the top four psychic clair senses that all Heavenly beings communicate through you with. Call on these Archangels for assistance in awakening that particular clair:

Archangel Uriel: Claircognizance (clear knowing)
Archangel Haniel: Clairsentience (clear feeling)
Archangel Zadkiel: Clairaudience (clear hearing)
Archangel Raziel: Clairvoyance (clear seeing)

CHAPTER THREE

*Ask for Divinely Guided
Angelic Help*

No one is ever truly in any kind of danger and all is always well in the end. You have Earthly life challenges that hinder your movement from day to day events such as getting your brakes fixed on your car. Now that's another expense you have to deal with. Other challenges such as figuring out how you're going to get out of work early to make it to your son's baseball game, to wondering if your love mate is cheating on you. You have larger challenges such as the death of a soul close to you leaving you to wonder how you'll continue on. A physical death is not the end as hard as that it is to accept and understand when moving through the grieving process. The soul simply moved onto more magnificent destinies that await it. Earthly life is the most limited restricting destiny that it truly is a soul relief to graduate from it.

Signs and symbols of angelic help is all around when you take the time to pay attention and notice it. The top important step is to ask for help, since no being in Heaven can intervene or offer assistance to anyone who doesn't ask for help. Some people may not believe that's possible or they have stopped believing, so they continue to suffer. It doesn't take much effort or time out of your day to stop what you're doing and ask for assistance from above. What do you have to lose by asking? If nothing else you've tried has helped, then what could it hurt to say the words?

Another step beyond asking for help is to be aware by paying attention to the repetitive action steps you may be guided to do. You might say, "I've asked for help and heard nothing."

Sometimes you're not going to hear the answer audibly or verbally. You might be given messages, answers, and guidance through nudges, signs, symbols, or other ways that can get your attention. Perhaps after you've asked for help you're invited to an event or party, but choose not to go because you're uncomfortable with social settings. You failed to notice the synchronicity that took place following you asking for heavenly guidance. Your Spirit team may have been orchestrating a meeting between you and another person who will be at this event. This other person could end up being someone that is connected to a future job you'll have, or they could be the next relationship partner or a new friend. Instead you chose to stay home alone when you were being asked to follow this guidance with an action step.

Asking for help can also entail asking another person for help since God and the angels also work through other people. You might be afraid to ask someone for assistance because you're shy or you don't want to bother or burden them. You might have a great deal of pride and are used to doing things yourself. Even the most self-sufficient person can use a hand occasionally. Sometimes the support can come in the form of helpful words of advice from another person. If you're down and out, then just talking to someone can be a great way to access support.

You might ask for Divine assistance, but then you start visualizing how you expect the answer to come in. The visualization soon forms into worry, which is a prayer killer. When you ask for help, step out of the way and busy yourself with other things. Meanwhile, allow the prayer request to come into your life the way it's supposed to on Divine timing. This is the same way you ask a friend or anyone else for help with anything, but then you end up getting frustrated. You then take over and do it yourself instead of allowing and trusting the other person to handle it in their own way. When you ask for Divine guidance or assistance, then let it go and step out of the way without interfering so God can handle it.

You could feel guilt or unworthiness about achieving success, which also creates a block. You see other successful people and the lower self part of you brings you down, "I'm nothing like them. Look at this woman. She's so good looking and this is why everyone is buying her products. And look at me, I don't have that look that people are attracted to."

Everyone has something of value to offer the public that helps them in some way. Looks will only get someone so far. Eventually looks fade, so if they don't have something else going for them, then they'll end up being a flash in the pan. Many have found this out the hard way. They were bowed down to for their looks in their twenties, but when they move into their thirties, forties, and beyond, they notice people are paying less attention to them. They discover society shuns or ignores them the way some do with older people on the sidewalk or in passing.

Abundance is not automatically granted to those that seek and ask for it. There are numerous factors that have to come into play. Sometimes life lessons and experience needs to happen before the rewards come in. Sitting around wishing and hoping for a miracle will generally not bring in the miracle. Tough times are part of the soul's growth process before the floodgates of abundance and blessings are cracked open.

You pray for help, follow the guidance coming

in, and then put in those action steps. Putting in action steps towards your goals can increase your odds of bringing in what you desire. This is due to a combination of factors from action movement to the positive excited feelings you have building up inside of you about the endeavor. The universe detects this optimistic energy you radiate outwardly. As you partake in endeavors that have a positive meaning for you, then playing an active role in the process will help over doing nothing. It's like the old saying that if you want to increase your chances to winning the lottery, then you have to buy a ticket. It doesn't mean you'll win the lottery, but you have more of a shot than if you didn't buy a ticket. This metaphor is similarly aligned with your dreams and goals coming to fruition.

If you don't ask for help, then how can the doorway to bring in help be forthcoming? Asking for help includes inviting in God and your Spirit team in your life to work with you daily. Working with you doesn't mean to grant all of your wishes. It is to guide you towards what you need to personally do to help move things along towards positive blessings. This includes the life lessons that will move you towards that doorway of light.

You can verbally ask for God and your Spirit team's help out loud, mentally in prayer, or you can write it out. It doesn't matter how you ask for heavenly help, but that you do. This is due to God's universal free will law that says no higher spirit being in Heaven can assist any soul unless they've been given permission to do so. This doesn't automatically mean that what you are asking for help with will happen or that it will happen right away. Be as clear as possible with your request, because your Spirit team follows what you ask for. If you are not specific, then you might be surprised by what comes in or doesn't come in. If the request sounds wishy-washy or unclear, then something else may come in that you don't want, or nothing at all will come in. You may even wonder why something came in that you didn't want, but then you recall what you asked for and realize that you indirectly requested it without realizing it.

Part of helping prayer requests along includes to think about what you'd like to have or what you'd like to accomplish. Visualize it happening in your mind, then put in daily practice of keeping it there. Let it overflow your entire body, mind, and soul with the essence of that desire. Make a pact to do this daily. You can do this at the start of the day upon waking, at night upon falling asleep or both. It won't hurt to do it more than once a day.

I was training with weights in a workout with a fitness friend. As I'm lifting I asked, "Should I do another rep?"

He said, "It can't hurt."

This is similar to making your dreams come true. It cannot hurt to give more than you typically give.

Don't worry about not asking for the right thing because requests are not automatically granted like Santa Claus with a sleigh full of gifts. If something is not aligned with your higher self, or if it's something bathed in greed, then it is unlikely to transpire. If it does, then it isn't long before something upsets that balance. This has been witnessed in cases where the greedy that achieve through deceitful means meet their demise at some point in their life.

Ask for help and have crystal clear intentions about what you desire. If you feel unsure of what you want, then this can create unsatisfactory results. If you fear asking for the wrong thing, then it is this fear that can manifest into a prayer block. Other blocks can be fear that you don't deserve help or fears of being selfish. Be sure of what you want and don't hold back for fear of asking for the wrong thing. Don't worry about whether or not your request is a selfish request or not. Your request may be selfish, but your Spirit team might not think so. If the request is considered selfish or not aligned with your souls' purpose, then the wish will unlikely be granted anyway.

Attracting in abundance and the laws of attraction believe that you can manipulate the energy in your life by the power of your own thoughts. It is much more complicated than that in Divine spiritual truth. The real truth is that if you work hard enough with persistence, passion, and optimism, and you couple that with prayer, then you have a far greater chance of achieving and reaching your goals. If you don't try, then you won't have a shot. If you battle with feeling depressed, worthless, or have low self-esteem, then the first steps will be to work on improving your well-being state. If your well-being state is perpetually in a negative state, then first focus on ways to improve that. This is not about someone who has the occasional drop down into negativity, but rather about those who battle uphill in life in that negative state every single day.

You can pray to God to improve your emotional state. If you're trying to accomplish something or you feel stuck and this is draining your life force, then pray to have your faith boosted and your emotional state brought to the heavenly dominated traits of love, joy, and peace.

Working on improving life's matters requires your dedication and persistence one day at a time through prayer and following the guidance given. You implement new strategies and techniques to apply to your life that help dissolve those negative feelings and thoughts you carry around. This is also why taking care of yourself on all levels possible is beneficial. It helps to keep you working on optimum levels while cracking open the psychic communication line with God. All of this is included as part of the process towards slamming that soul enlightenment door wide open.

CHAPTER FOUR

*Turn Prayers
Into Manifestation*

We are in a critical state as a human race. Many are unhappy with where they are at in their lives attempting to reach for a miracle or an answered prayer. You wake up in the morning and your mind immediately moves into worry or something negative. You know how this makes you feel and it's not pleasant. This is how you have set the tone and theme for your day. I have certainly had those moments in my past. Every morning my eyes open I move into a Divine channel and communicate with God and my Spirit team.

I may ask them, "Is there anything I need to know right now or is there anything you would like to discuss?"

I will also let them know what I am grateful and thankful for. This is followed by positive affirmations, which have a higher frequency vibration when you say them.

Read this line: "I'm broke and never have any money."

How does that feel to you? It feels heavy doesn't it? I felt that just writing it. Well, guess what you're summoning? You're bringing in more of that broke stuff to you.

How about instead you say something like: "I have plenty of money flowing into my world that never stops. I am taken care of and my needs are met in all ways."

Notice how saying that makes you feel.

Your lower self is the imposter self that will chime in at about this moment.

"Yeah, well I don't have a lot of money. I wish."

The Darkness will feed you self-deprecating thoughts such as, "I'll never get that job. I'm too old. I'm too fat. They want someone younger and better looking."

When the Darkness and lower self runs the show that is your life, then it seeks to undo the greatness that you were born with. It does not want to see you happy or succeed. Whereas God and your higher self knows there is plenty to go around and works with you to ensure you are taken care of and guided to circumstances that bring you closer to hitting gold.

When you say something like, "I'm never going

to get that job." Then it feels as if there is a heavy weight of an elephant sitting on you. It makes you feel low and worthless, which subsequently begins to bring in that same energy into your life. What spirals in is a domino effect of more negative things that only increase those feelings of low self-worth.

Now firmly say believing it: "I WILL get that job."

Much better.

Now say: "I HAVE this job, and all is wonderful."

Even better!

Say it as if you have it and mean it. Even if you don't have it yet, say it every day as if you do. Never stop saying it or believing it. This is what a positive affirmation is. It trains your mind to be in that space more than when it's not.

The main aspects where people struggle the most are the areas of career, love, finances, home life and health. These are the areas that people often want to look at when they get a reading or consultation with a professional. It's no surprise that they are all connected to physical human survival and happiness, so it's understandable to long for those basic human desires. It's difficult to comprehend that in order to begin reaching those physical desires, one must start within by working on their soul's consciousness and change their perception and outlook while including a boost in faith.

When you fight needlessly against the current, then your circumstances grow worse. This is due to the energy you are putting out there. Because your soul often feels trapped in human form in this heavy and dense atmosphere, your lower self and ego rises and becomes attracted to material and superficial things. Your soul is limited in its body for a reason, but the angels, guides and spirit souls are unlimited. You lose yourself in outside events forgetting who and what you are.

If you use negative affirmations, thoughts, words and feelings, then you end up bringing more of that negativity to you. You are always manifesting throughout your life whether you want to or like it or not, so you may as well manifest what you want. Use positive affirmations and words when you speak, think, or write so that you can attract that same energy in. Try it out for a week and observe how things improve for you. You will discover that this will take practice since no one likes to try to be happy. That takes too much effort. It isn't long before the ego grows angry attempting to take over once again. It doesn't matter if your ego fights you on it. Because you can train your higher self to take it right back. Always revert to seeing things as working out positively in your life in amazing ways.

Perhaps you've experienced a situation where your work life is on cloud nine, while another part of your life suffers, such as love and relationships. It may feel like one area of your life is mastered while the other areas are lacking in positivity. If you excel and shine with confidence whenever you are at work, then this is a great example of where it comes to you naturally. This state is a positive form of manifesting. Your lower self does not question it or think about pulling you down. This is the same as creating a vision or dream board. You are saying the magic words without realizing it.

Look at how self-assured you are when you are at work or doing what you love. You can do it effortlessly and blissfully. This is the state where you manifest positive circumstances in other areas of your life. You have the positive visions and attitude in your mind and know how to accomplish what you need to when you are at work. This is how I obtained the things I wanted in my work life. I saw it in my mind's eye beforehand, even though it would seem impossible to someone else at the time. I prayed on it and asked for repetitive help. I knew and felt it in my gut and every cell of my body that what I was asking for WILL happen. I paid no mind to anything else including the critics or my lower self, and I eventually obtained what was envisioned and asked for.

Never discredit the power of prayer. I've spoken to others that have no belief in prayer. They do not believe in God or that there is any kind of higher power, or they may not pray because their prayers had never been answered before, so they gave up on that. However, those same people may suddenly call out to God when something detrimental happens to them or to someone close to them. God notices that you will cry out for him suddenly in a panic. He wants you to always communicate with Him, and not only when there is a dire circumstance begging for His intervention.

He wishes to have a closer relationship with you beyond only needing help.

Prayer has provided miracles over the centuries to millions of people. I have witnessed the marvels and wonders that have taken place by praying. It is not enough to pray, but to keep an optimistic mindset and take action steps where you're guided. If you pray, but continue to fall into deeper despair, then pray for help with your emotional state. Once your emotional state is back to full power, then you are in that space where you can pray with detachment for the outcome of your desires.

Pray with intention, which means you are experiencing the prayer coming true through all parts of your soul and physical body. Prayers are also positive affirmations contrary to some beliefs. The positive affirmations have an even more powerful effect when you work with God on the affirmations.

For example, "Thank you God for empowering me to do what you've called my soul to do."

It does not matter how you pray or whether you recite positive affirmations. It all has the same energy intention. God, the angels, and your guides are with you hearing every word.

There is no wrong way to pray. Traditional religions have shown one often depicted as kneeling down by a bed with their hands clasped together while others may bow. It does not matter how or where you do it, but that you do it. Prayer is great because it can be done from anywhere. You can communicate with God mentally in prayer as you are walking to your car to driving or sitting at a spotlight. Of course, you won't have your eyes closed and hands clasped together in those cases. You are building a stronger relationship with the Divine through prayer. It is beyond praying when nothing is going right in your life, but it is praying to acknowledge when things are going right.

Prayers are communicating to God and your Spirit team out loud, mentally, or in writing. Prayers are asking for help or thanking God and your Spirit team for their assistance. Praying is praying for other people too! You do not want to be slacking in that department either. If someone is cruel to you, it is easy to want to lash out or become negatively affected. Try praying for that person instead. Request that they receive intervention and assistance to find the love that exists somewhere within and operate from their higher self.

Atheists have protested that they do not believe in prayer. They may however sit with their own thoughts and ponder about their life at some point. They will feel grateful for what they have, what is to come, or what they would like to have. Without realizing it they are praying in those instances. They are reciting or conducting positive affirmations and prayer. It is the same concept and intent regardless of what title you use to describe it within your personal belief systems. All thoughts, affirmations, or prayers are heard by God and your Spirit team depending on what it is.

A non-believer might say something like, "How

can they talk to someone in the sky who does not exist?"

To them He does not exist, but to others He does. I do not blindly know that He, my Guides or Angels exist. I have experienced great circumstances firsthand by being connected to them since I was born. This was by repeatedly testing them out whenever possible. I have requested specific Divine assistance only to witness it come true not long afterwards. I've tested them by saying, "I'm going to test you on this."

They would then make the small request happen to give me that boosted faith that the larger requests that are taking forever are being worked on. I am always communicating with Him daily and subsequently receiving results. If I never did, then I wouldn't bother with prayer.

Prayers are not always answered in the way you expect or hope. Sometimes they are answered in another way you never thought of. When it comes to all things beyond the physical world it is important to keep an open mind. You can add in your prayer requests that you wish for a desire to come to fruition pending that it will not put you in danger or cause more issues. I have mentally asked for help in prayer, and then watched it eventually come to fruition. Sometimes it is immediately and sometimes it is far off in the distance, but I never stop praying or believing. I know that there are reasons that nothing is happening right away, because there are certain pieces of the puzzle that have to come into place first.

Many long for practical security-based things because this is a physical world that requires those necessities to survive or make life a bit more bearable. Let's say that you are wondering why the right love partner has not come into your life yet. It may be that you are ready, but perhaps your love partner is in a place where they are not ready to meet you yet. They may currently be involved with someone that will not last. It might also be that you're not ready and have more soul growth work that will bring you to the level of the partner that God wants to bring you. Keep an open mind and consider all the possibilities as to why certain prayer requests are not coming to fruition.

Always say thank you for being helped as well, and not just I need I need. The angels love it when you show gratitude and express thanks for what you currently have. You don't want to become a spoiled child of God who takes and asks constantly. You are blessed in many ways so take time out to say thank you. Every morning when I'm getting ready for the day I'm communicating with my Guides and Angels. There is not a day that goes by where I am not. Some of the things I say to them are things like, "Thank you for my health, thank you for the place I live in, etc."

I move down the list letting them know how grateful I am for the blessings I currently have. I feel more alive and alert when I start my sentences with, "Thank you for…."

Those words have ferocious power!

Focus on being grateful and saying thank you for

what you have and watch how much lighter and happier you start to feel. You'll find that your life starts to feel less tumultuous in the process. Being grateful and saying thank you raises your soul's vibration and consciousness to the level where positive Divinely guided manifestation occurs. Your prayers are ultimately answered in ways that benefit your higher self. You may need to get knocked around off your high horse a bit and dragged through the mud before you can see your prayer answered.

It seems challenging to break out of a cycle of negative thoughts and words used. It feels far easier to think and speak negative thoughts and worry. How about saying something positive? Choose not to live your life in misery. Basking in God's love helps one live with gratitude and more joy. Choose not to allow your lower self to have control over you dominating your thoughts and mood.

You can pray for other people and send angels to intervene with someone else, but that person has to also want help. The angels will definitely be by their side. They will give them love, offer assistance and nudges, but if that person is not paying attention or wanting it, then there is only so much that can be done. God and the angels will stay by that person's side continuously trying to get them to notice. They do not give up on you, but do you just give up?

Here are some examples of positive affirmations and high vibrational phrases:

"I am worthy."

"I have strong health."

"I am loved."

"I have a financially successful career."

"I live in a beautiful house in the countryside."

"I have a loving and loyal relationship partner."

"My opinion is just as valid as anyone else's."

"I am taken care of in all ways."

Don't shortchange yourself or be embarrassed as if you are not deserving of a great life. Heaven and your angels know you deserve it. They want you to be at peace so that you can fulfill your life purpose. You do not have to be on this planet to suffer indefinitely.

Make a list with your own positive affirmations and recite it every day either mentally or out loud. Do it before bed or when you wake up. Keep doing it until you have obtained your dreams. God, the angels and spirituality are like vitamins. You have to keep at it daily before you begin to notice the much-needed improvement and changes shifting in your life.

Everything you desire will not happen right away. Sometimes for certain things there are life lessons that you must go through and be enlightened about on your own before the next step is shown. If you are feeling stuck at a dead-end job and nothing is moving forward, then look at the lesson that is surrounding where you are at and acknowledge this. To do this you have to be completely unbiased and remove your ego from the equation. Look at this dead-end job in a positive light and ask yourself, "What have I learned while I have been here? How am I being of service to others while there?"

What positive trait or traits did you gain while working this particular job that you did not have before? This is your answer to absorb and learn from. Acknowledge it so that you are open and ready for your next step.

You can write to your angels about anything you want in a prayer. This is by writing it to them in a notepad or in an email that you email to yourself. Tell them about your fears, issues, and circumstances you would like to change. When you pour your heart out to them with great purpose and intention, then you are truly heard. Then release it and move on with living life graciously and positively. Have patience with the outcome. Watch the miracles and changes happen in the coming months that follow as you continue with this positive mindset.

When you pray or recite positive affirmations, I will conclude it with: "This - or something better God."

Because they may have something greater than you imagined in mind and you don't want to limit yourself. Your dreams and wishes come true, but sometimes not the way you requested. It will be in an even greater way than you expected. It can be a major change, or it can be subtle. Sometimes you will find you're still at the workplace you complained about, but then you realize that you're perfectly content there. They are keeping you somewhere for a reason and to fulfill a purpose such as getting along with a particular colleague. The delays can be that they have much to maneuver beforehand or have a grander plan that you cannot see yet.

Remain optimistic and open minded to the outcome of your prayers. Know that there is a reason for everything that is happening for you in your life at any particular time. Know that you also have the power to change that simply by adjusting the way you think and feel about it.

Ask and you shall receive. Pray about the changes you'd like to see happen in your life. Have faith and believe in it. Focus only on what you desire to see happen and not what you don't want. For example, say something like, "Please guide me to friendships with like-minded interests."

Also add in, "Thank you."

Be grateful for what you have.

"Thank you for keeping my body healthy in all ways. I'm grateful that I have shelter, etc."

Shifting your outlook can take practice and time, but before you know it, you will start noticing the positive changes happening in your life.

Ask Archangel Michael and/or Jesus Christ to surround you with white light protecting you from lower energies when you pray. Praying for others has therapeutic effects. When you send positive words about someone else whether in the form of a prayer, affirmation, or a statement, then you are raising your soul's energy vibration. This process not only results in additional healing light sent to the other person, but this same light is magnified and re-directed back onto yourself as well. This only solidifies the theory that your thoughts do produce things to an extent, whether those thoughts are of yourself or someone else.

When someone upsets you and you find yourself complaining about them, you are not only sending negative energy to that person, but that energy you're toying with acts as a mirror reflecting the same energy right back onto your soul. Many have admitted that when doing that they noticed it was one negative thing after another preceding that. This is why it is important to catch yourself when you discover that you are spending more time using negative words about a situation and quickly modify them to be optimistic. Sending prayers or positive words to someone else is a win-win situation because it not only has the added benefit of elevating the other person's soul, but it also improves yours.

Sending positive prayers and affirmations to others will help as much as the other person allows it to. They have free will choice to go against the prayers and override any heavenly assistance offered. If they are choosing to stay in a negative space or they're making choices that their ego insists on, then there is little you or Heaven can do. When you send prayers to another person, the angels will continue to uplift that person's thoughts and nudge them in the right direction continuously hoping that person will notice.

Sometimes you pray for change with little to no instant results. When you notice that nothing has happened, your ego kicks in and causes you to worry. The ego wants things immediately. You start to lose faith when you notice nothing has changed. Your unanswered prayers sometimes have other factors that need to come into play first before you notice changes.

There are times when your prayers are answered. The way it is answered might not be in the manner you expect it. You fail to notice the blessings that have indeed trickled into your life. There are the repeated signs you ignore that your Spirit team is asking you to do. It could be something as simple as signing up to take a particular class or go to a location you're guided to. They put these Divine signs in front of you. For example, you might notice that you continue to notice the same seminar flyer, but you never act on it or equate it to Divine orchestration. Sometimes your Spirit team has to maneuver certain pieces of the puzzle before you notice the changes. Other times they want you to endure a particular experience as part of your karmic thread, life lesson, and soul's growth. The insight you gain in what appears to be a less than stellar situation carries over into your new situation. You have the revelation of why the experience was necessary, then it all eventually makes sense.

A Prayer

"I'd like to thank God for creating this planet and its entire habitat, plants, wildlife, animals and the beauty of all of the nature surroundings. Help me to take care of it and never take it or my life for granted. Thank you for providing me with all of the necessities I need to survive in a human body such as food, clothing, housing and finances. Help me to align perfectly with my higher self and its purpose while here. Thank you for assisting me to revert to living in and expressing love full time."

CHAPTER FIVE

*Create an Abundant Life
With Faith*

Having an abundant life can mean many things to different people. It can be something that makes you happy and gives you daily pleasure. It can be filled with good positive-minded friends that accept you unconditionally no matter how many skeletons you reveal. There is nothing you can say that would make them write you off. Your mutual loyalty is sacrament to the both of you. I would be the first to help a friend bury the body, which I know select people can truly jokingly say that and mean it. Especially today where people are quickly writing one another off if a flaw is revealed or if their choices are not exactly like yours. If they vote politically a certain way or have a different spiritual view, you could be kicked out of someone's life with the snap of a finger. They quickly write others off when what they believe to be any imperfection is revealed. That's not mafia like loyalty at all, but a loyalty riddled with conditions. Having that kind of rigid stance with your own clan will ensure the instability continues on in other areas. This attitude blocks the positive flow of abundance from coming in.

Some of my best friends may partake or have participated in behavior that I don't condone, but I don't write them off. Accepting people's differences takes an immense amount of work. No one is exactly like anybody else and people are going to do things or believe in things that are disagreeable to you. How you choose to accept that and not take it personally can have an effect on how successfully you navigate through those Earthly life hiccups and challenges. One of the repeated phrases I've heard from friends and those around me are, "I feel I can always tell you anything and you don't have any judgment at all. I don't know anyone else that's like that."

An abundant life today can be about having more good times, fun, and laughter. Laughter raises your vibration up into God's vortex. You can feel your vibration has risen when this happens. Your vibration is your overall well-being and energetic state. Your physical self and spiritual self work in tandem with one another. If you're feeling low, then your vibration is low. If you're on cloud nine and filled with happiness, then your vibration is high.

You've likely had one of those laughing fits at some point in your life. You were also able to detect how that made you feel, and the feeling was good. You could feel it through your entire being. Suddenly you were walking on clouds happy in life. Some have commented that they could sense that infectious wonder just by hearing someone else's laughing fit in the vicinity. Maybe it happened while you were at a restaurant, in a movie theater, or at work. You smile and look at whomever you're with and share a telepathic acknowledgment that this laughing fit you're hearing is irresistible.

The laughter and joy are an example of what raises your soul vibration. When your vibration is raised, then it reaches that threshold where abundance and blessings flow in. This is why it's important to bring these little things up as reminders as to what can help in accelerating the flow of good things in your life. It doesn't mean you're going to be drama and challenge free.

God can mean diverse things to different people from a higher power, the Light, Spirit, the Universe, and so on. My own life was less dramatic and less challenging when I devoted my life to God full time. It included incorporating these little tips to the point that I noticed a grander shift happening. It was too obvious not to notice the positive changes and results that were surfacing.

An abundant life can be about partaking in work that excites you and brings out your passions. This is also similar to finding your life purpose and diving wholeheartedly into that in the right spirit. It enables you to have enough time outside of that work you do to spend with friends, family, and loved ones, or whatever activities you find pleasurable. This is pending it's not harming you or another person.

Some find anything associated with the word pleasure to be evil. You're not intended to have a miserable life. Pleasures and playtime fun are essential in making sure you're not overloaded with constant stress or that you don't experience burnout. This isn't about the kinds of pleasures that are considered toxic, dangerous, or unhealthy. It might be to go on a hike with a friend, or a fun road trip to a destination far enough away from home to feel as if you're getting away, but close enough to get to. It can be that you have enough time to take regular breaks and see places you've always wanted to visit and explore. It can be watching a movie that entertains, inspires, and helps you escape a hard circumstance for a spell. It can be spending intimate time with a lover. You have that beautiful blissful loving soul union relationship with someone, which makes your life feel abundant.

Having an abundant life can be having enough income to be able to live problem and worry free without fear of never being able to pay your bills or purchase practical necessities to survive. You've reached that place in your life where you are no longer struggling. You can choose the area you've always wanted to live in. You can buy that home of your dreams. You can and may even obtain all of that and much more, but you may still feel unfulfilled. Without a strong spiritual connection with something greater than yourself, you can be left feeling empty even after achieving and obtaining those material physical pleasures and desires. There are countless cases of people who fought hard to achieve materialistic abundance, but were still left feeling just as empty as they were before obtaining those things.

Some people seek out and chase fame and fortune. They achieve that and more in a big way, but have admitted to still feeling empty, low, unimpressed and unsatisfied. There are similar cases reported where someone was chasing material physical pleasures and desires. This is because true authentic happiness and joy comes from within rather than what you can get your physical hands onto. The latter kinds of happiness are short lived and operate more like a drug that might satisfy for a quick moment, but then like any drug the high soon wears off and you're left where you started.

Many purported to say they found that happiness in a strong spiritual connection, whether that is a connection with Jesus, Buddha, God, the Universe, or Spirit. It doesn't matter what you call it even though in some spiritual circles they may do their best to make you feel guilty or bad, and might even bully you for not following who they personally follow. This is not about them or what they want for you. This has been especially the case in extreme organized fundamentalist religious organizations. That behavior is what has chased followers and people away from those systematic human made created religions. Because of their self-righteous and judgment on others claiming they are doing it out of love, they have pushed people away from Christ and the Churches. Now people hear the name Jesus Christ and they cringe. They assume he is the one casting the judgment, when his love is all love. The harsh judgment casting was coming from his misinformed followers that wallow in the darkness of ego. Out of thousands of pages in a book, they only follow a few passages that were added at a later date during a superstitious time. They only use those passages to use as ammunition to attack and condemn others. This is not being spiritual or of Christ. You are a flawed human being and every soul will transform and evolve on their own timing. Forcing them to do that will never end well.

Statistics have popped up showing a never-ending decrease in religious followers because of all of this. They've chased some people to the further extreme of atheism. Although now more people today are finding a stronger connection with God in the spiritual communities, which angers extreme religious followers and atheists. Extremist religious people have great disdain for anyone that is not strictly and religiously following the Bible word for word, even though many of them cherry pick and choose what they want to follow themselves anyway. They will use the excuse that it is okay as long as they ask God for forgiveness for their wicked ways.

There are a great number of people that walk in both worlds of the spiritual and religious. They are some of the most content and centered people I've met because of that balance. They might praise Jesus while being supportive of people no matter their race, political affiliation, gender, sexual orientation, and on and on.

Some of the extreme sides of spirituality or religious disagree with someone being able to walk in both worlds, but that just means they're unable to or choose not to. They don't have a say in what you decide is best for you. This is your life and when you walk with God, you are able to be more of an efficient manager and owner of that life. No one else can claim that power, even if they use the Bible as an excuse to justify their insistence on you changing to bend to their ways. They don't have the market cornered on what God wants for you. It is your journey to discover God's ultimate purpose and guidelines for you.

Regardless of your spiritual beliefs, you are trained early on by society and your peers, to achieve a high status of popularity and fortune. Some abundance teachers and motivational preachers ask you to pay large amounts of money and sign up for their seminars so that you too can work where you want and still have enough time to travel the world freely. People chase those practical monetary dreams only to find that it never pans out that way. While a small percentage might achieve it, they continue to fight to achieve more physical desires long after the achievement. Many remain unhappy and stressed out throughout life. They haven't figured out that this is not working for them. They're unhappy because they're merely going along with what they were trained early on to seek. At the same time, you understand the need or desire to at least be making enough of an income that you can live comfortably without fear of not being able to pay your bills.

Perhaps you have a large calling and purpose guiding you to partake in work that is not only your passion, but it is a purpose that has a snowball positive side effect of helping others. The problem is you don't have enough time to devote to it, because you work a full-time day job that does not fulfill you in any way. You want to quit that job so you can participate in the work that means something to you. You can't quit that day job because you need an income to be able to pay your rent, buy food, clothing, and practical necessities. You know you have to quit in order to focus solely on your passions and life purpose, but that is not a realistic move, so you wind up feeling stuck. You could look for another job to get out of the life force draining one, but you also know you may end up moving from one poor circumstance to another.

Money doesn't solve the problems of happiness, but it does help to have enough to physically survive. And in that scenario described, having enough income where you don't need to work a time and energy sucking full time day job with toxic people is not an outlandish desire for a physical being.

The good news is there is a glimmer of light at the end of that dark tunnel. Devoting just a small amount of time each day or week towards your passions that you desire to be lucrative can give you something to look forward to. There are many success stories where someone lived that way and reaped in positive benefits. Add to that daily prayer and asking for heavenly guidance gives this a greater shot and making this dream come true.

There are also stories about those who were in a situation like that for years. They worked hard on their passion and purpose on the side while at a day job they despised. Once enough of a steady income was coming in with that passion purpose side work, they were able to comfortably quit their day job without fear or worry, and partake in the work that truly is their passion and love.

Regardless of what your finances are like, you are the manager and creator of your life. When you team up with God and your Spirit team, then there is no telling what you can accomplish. You can decide how you will act or react to something someone says or does. You can choose the job you want to look for to an extent. Sometimes you may end up accepting a job you don't really want because you have bills to pay. You are still choosing to make that temporary sacrifice by accepting that blessing of a job. No one is putting a gun to your head. You are doing the best you can in managing your life with the resources you have at this juncture in your life.

Achieving a utopian abundance life state is what the soul desires because it reminds it of home where everything was blissful and peaceful. It's like you moved from a mansion overlooking paradise in Heaven to a rundown apartment on Earth for a brief time in your soul's existence. You did so for the sake of evolving your soul. Your soul doesn't evolve much unless it has to endure rough experiences for the purpose of lessons learned.

When you learn a lesson on Earth, then that means you learned from the mistake. When you learn from a mistake, you grow and work on not doing it again. Some get stuck in that cycle of repeating the same mistakes until they notice the pattern and snap out of it. This way they can move onward and forward.

Even the most miserable person on the planet longs for happiness deep down inside the core of their soul. Happiness being subjective since one person's version of the happiness they desire could differ from another ones.

There are people who have evil fantasies of world domination and that would make them happy. This of course is not the kind of abundance God and my Spirit team speaks of or the kind you're even thinking about. This is also what they mean when they say happiness is individual based.

One person could desire a home, the love soul mate marriage partner, the kids, and a good job. Those requests would fulfill their physical desires. For another they may not care about any of that, but want the freedom as a single person to roam about the world and travel to see the different parts of the globe and dive into higher culture learning.

Longing for that authentic abundant life feeling starts from within. You fill yourself up with overflowing happy thoughts of Divinely guided enlightenment and abundance. Your emotional state feels like you're riding sky high above the clouds. It's to live a utopian existence that would be possible if people acted from their better nature and fought to function through life in a high vibrational state. Most of the chaos and turmoil created is at the hands of other people or conjured up within you. Your goal should be to reach this utopian paradise state, but then transcend even higher than that. When you are in the epicenter of that vibrational energy, then there is no telling what kind of bountiful abundance would come flowing in.

CHAPTER SIX

*Increase Faith to Accomplish,
Achieve, and Persevere*

Craving human interaction and social stimulation is something sought out by many, while other people prefer to function alone. When you have a strong connection with God and Spirit, then you never feel lonely. Loneliness is ultimately longing for a connection to fulfill you that can only truly be satisfied by God. To have a mutually reciprocated blissful love union with another person is to know God, because a soul's best qualities are parts of Him.

Since it's sometimes difficult for a human soul to have a connection with God, the ego part of one's self will crave love, attention, and admiration from other people. It's temporarily fulfilling because no one can ever fill that space within you except God. God in this case is not that cliché image of a man with a beard sitting on a chair in the sky. This is the image that non-believers tend to overuse, which has no basis in the reality of the massive energy force that created all that IS.

All souls desire some form of companionship with at least one person. Some people might disagree, but they do crave some form of a relationship based in love if even through a social circle of friends.

A businessman might say that he only cares about work and money, yet he is cut off from the Universe and the Divine. If he didn't have to get it from some source connected to another person, then he wouldn't crave it at all. He needs other people around him. If they weren't around and all people were taken away from him so that he could be completely alone, then it wouldn't be long before he begins to go crazy and start to miss that stimulation and crave another person.

If this businessman showed up on Earth to find no other people, then he wouldn't know what he was missing. Because there is no material distraction he would be more in tune to the Heavens unable to hear anything else. This is how human beings progressed in the beginning of civilization. They paid attention to the Heavens and their Divine senses to guide them on how to naturally progress.

Eventually it expanded and exploded to the point of never-ending distractions. The more this chaos rose up, the less Divinely connected human beings became. There is no way to escape that and not be aware that it's happening, even if you live in the middle of nowhere. While you might be more connected to Spirit in those areas, you lose the connection when you turn your television on, you surf the internet, you read media stories, or partake in toxic timewasters. Now you are no longer spiritually connected.

You might be connected to one another through technological devices, but in a distant loveless way. You are not connected to God through those forms. The entire planet is unsettled making it near impossible to sense the Divine energy that way. Your subconscious is aware of it, even if you're not paying attention to it in the present moment. If you're a highly spiritually connected being, then you're versed and readily able to move in and out of the Spirit connection whenever it calls for it.

Your soul's life force dies little by little living a life you're unhappy with. Perhaps you feel emotionally dead as if you don't have much else to give anymore. You've asked for help for years and became doubtful that it will ever happen at this point. You're waiting, hoping, praying, and taking action for years wondering if a miracle and blessings will reveal itself to you. It can make you doubt, lose faith, and question if there is a God. It sounds like a roller coaster ride of voices competing with one another from your ego to your angels, to your ego, to your angels.

I love films from all genres, from horror, to intense dramas, to frat boy comedies, and to films with an uplifting spiritually based message like, *The*

Shack.

In *The Shack*, the character Mack is a Man that grew up in a home full of physical and emotional abuse. As a Father in present day, one of his youngest daughters is abducted by a serial killer that rapes and kills her. Something this extreme and bleak had to take place so that viewers can understand how this man's faith and trust in God and life are gone.

He endures emotional and mental anguish, horror, anger, and a loss of spirit. He's led to the shack where his daughter was killed by who he believes is the killer. He's in for a powerful awakening when he discovers it's the Holy Trinity, but taking the form of people. Jesus and the Holy Spirit are there along with God Himself, who takes the form of a woman.

The man is confused and says to God, "Do I know you?"

God chuckles, "Not very well." And then with firm inviting comfort, "But we can work on that."

I loved the film from that point when the man gets to hang out and develop a stronger relationship with the Holy Trinity. They take the form of a warm cozy family that feels like a Hallmark card feeding you spiritual wisdom that isn't that far off from the truth. Through this relationship, they help this man regain his faith and hope in himself and life again.

Some strict religious people found this to be heresy, while some non-believers found it to be like a church sermon. As usual, I don't hang on either side and found *The Shack* to be uplifting, truthful, with a Universal message of love. It feels like taking a warm bath in the Paradise of Light with Heaven's greats that is moving, joyful and empowering.

Focus on your Soul's Purpose

When your consciousness is raised, it is not uncommon to feel disconnected from other people and view human life as trivial. This is when it's time to do an inventory check of how the months and years to date have gone for you. Examine your triumphs, sorrows, successes, and challenges. What was lost and what was gained throughout that time. You'd be surprised to find the hidden blessings you never thought much of until you look back on it. When things are going amazingly, people don't usually notice it as much as they do when things are going horribly. One can take it for granted until you take a moment to note, "Okay, my rent gets paid every month, my health is great, and I have a working car that gets me to my job."

Look forward to the coming time up ahead with promise and hope. Believe your life will get better and accept nothing less than that. Celebrate your wins and accomplishments to acknowledge what you've done. This also helps lighten the burdens of life that you experience on occasion.

Success comes and goes the way fame comes and goes. One of the best dreams to come true is being able to turn your love and hobby into a financially lucrative career. You are closer than someone else might be if you understand the concept of manifestation and asking for what you want. If you're stressed out at your job regularly, then is the job worth it? Make wise choices in your life that do not result in leaving you in a bind where you're perpetually unhappy. This might mean taking a job for less pay and living beneath your typical means until you find the work that makes you feel bliss again.

Looking to the future with optimism you might sometimes find you've been chasing rainbows that evaporate as quickly as the champagne fizzles in your glass. You need not search long and hard for some measure of magic to reveal itself since it's always resided within you. You are loved by God even when you doubt it, avoid it, shun it and do everything in your power to deny it. When you reach that threshold of completing your Earthly run, the only thing you take with you is love. If you gain anything while here, then remember to love more, give more, and have compassion no matter how unpopular it is. Only then can you truly discover that magic you secretly desire.

Keep a journal for a month and write down every single thing that bothers you. This means a trending topic you found yourself falling into. After enough time has passed revert back to that journal to see what you wrote. Notice if it has truly had any positive effect on changing your life, or if it was just another time waster you fell emotionally drawn to, but could care less about months later. It will be mind boggling to witness the long list of time wasters that prevented you from being happy and moving forward.

Focus on your life purpose rather than time wasters that act as a procrastination technique to prevent you from getting to work on what you desire. The tiny action steps you make are creating change even if you don't feel like it is while in the midst of it. You may think that someone else will take care of an issue, but no one really is or does. If you need to go it alone, then you have to go it alone and tackle it one issue at a time. One small action step can get the energy flowing in that direction. Research and seek out ways that change can be made in the area of your interest that you strongly feel needs to be changed.

Sometimes healthy time wasters have good mind enhancing properties, such as those card games like Solitaire or emailing or texting friends back to get you out of a procrastination cycle. You just want to make sure you don't fall too deep into the time wasters that you find four hours have passed and you have yet to get to work on your dreams. Even just a small amount of time working on action steps that can one day bring you what you desire will make all the difference in the world. It's definitely more advantageous than contributing nothing towards it. As always follow this all up with regular insistent prayer knowing that something good will happen for you.

CHAPTER SEVEN

Complaining Into Abundance

There is the reality that you may not have a choice and will have to accept what is coming your way. This is part of the physical survival on Earth, but one that is also contributing to your soul's growth and evolving process. This may come in the form of accepting any job position to ensure your security. You have to do what you need to do in order to stay afloat without worry.

During my day job tenure, I accepted any old job that I wasn't all that happy with, but they did give me some measure of flexibility. It was close to home and the safety net of that job enabled me to find an even better job that I truly wanted months later.

When you feel worry and stress over your day

job, or not having enough money to work on your life purpose, then you risk moving into worry or complaining territory. Complaining is an abundance, prayer, and blessing killer. If you spend your life complaining, you will guarantee that you will be given more to complain about.

Several of my friends and I have a pact where we step in if we see someone falling into perpetual complaining. This is pointed out to help one another stop the runaway train downwards. This is not done insensitively or to quiet one's voice from expressing itself. It also doesn't mean ignoring a problem one is experiencing. This is about taking a step back to evaluate what can be done about the issue that is causing the person to complain for days, weeks, and sometimes months.

When you are fearful about something, then it will cause you to vent and complain about that. This isn't telling you to suppress your worries and fears, but rather get to the level of realizing when it's happening, have your quick complaint about it, but then shift that into something positive like an action step that can be done to help move out of that dirty cycle of complaining.

When I've prayed or asked for Divine assistance, then that was when the assistance eventually came. I wouldn't force-feed you prayer if it never worked for me. When your thoughts move into a plea or gratitude, then you've moved into prayer. You might call it an affirmation or just something you were thinking about, but it is a prayer that the Universe and Heaven are hearing come out of you. They will also hear you when you're incessantly complaining whether out loud or to anyone listening. Complaining that nothing is happening or changing for you will not suddenly bring in the blessings.

Complaining your way into blessings and abundance will not result in success. If you're going to continue complaining about something, then don't bother praying for it since the complaint will negate the prayer anyway. You ask for heavenly help, but nothing comes around as quick as you'd like it if at all, so you assume you've been given up on. You might play the victim card that no one was able to help, you're being ignored, and woe is me. God is attempting to train you to stand tall, pull yourself up by your bootstraps, and forge forward fearlessly with faith as your anchor. When you pass on you're not taking anyone or anything with you. You will be making the journey home solo with the exceptions of God and your Spirit team that are ushering you into the Light.

Learn to get to know and lean on your Spirit team for assistance when your faith and well-being are wavering. Work on being grateful for the blessings they've helped you with to date. Do you have clothes, food, and a roof over your head? Then say, "Thank you."

Some people are under the impression that the job of heavenly helpers is to grant your desires like a genie in a bottle. When that doesn't happen you automatically assume they must not exist, or you're being ignored. You're expected to participate and do the work yourself as well too. Sitting around on your couch drinking a beer all day watching a sports game hoping gifts will fall from the ceiling onto your sofa is never going to happen just because you've asked for it. It's also not Heaven's job or anyone else's job to constantly tell you what to do, where to go, and when to do it. It's your job to do those things. You're given what you need, not necessarily what you want. Needs are the essentials such as housing, food, and clothing.

Spirit guides will step in when necessary to nudge you to move in a certain direction where the most benefit for your soul's growth exists. They will not live your life for you. You're not a puppet on a string that they're controlling. They are like any good best friend who taps you on the shoulder to get you to notice something important, but it's not their burden to carry if you fail to detect it. They can put the same repetitive cues in front of you to get you to see something, but there's nothing more they can do if you're not paying attention to it. If you don't make moves and go after what you want, then nothing will happen because they are not going to do it for you. If you don't have the confidence to go after what you want, then confidence gaining skills is one of your life purposes to master. This can also be added to your prayer requests, which is to help be given more confidence. Avoiding an action step towards making something happen is something you must learn to overcome and master.

Complaining is surrounded with undesirable energy that lowers your soul's vibration and opens the gate for the Darkness to ensnare in its trap that block even more goodness. Negative anything will manifest into health-related concerns down the line. Sometimes you fall into perpetual daily complaining that you don't even realize you are doing that because it's become habitual.

If everything that comes out of you is toxic or a harsh assaulting judgment, then that energy will grow and manifest into more of the same. It marinates into the cells and pores of your physical, emotional, and spiritual body making you permanently one with it. You may know someone like that, and you know they're a challenging person to be around.

The largest culprits put that energy out into the Universe by posting words aligned with toxicity on their social media accounts. They're not aware that the Darkness has enveloped them. Having an understanding that the person can no longer help it can offer some measure of light in how you navigate around someone like that. The best thing to do is avoid or ignore them as much as possible. This is unless absolutely necessary such as in the workplace where you have no choice but to face them. Limit contact to work related dialogue in those instances. Being around someone who is perpetually negative and toxic will affect you, your energy, and vibration. This has an effect on how things go in your life by negating the positive process from working in your favor. Call in the Archangel Michael to extricate toxic people from your vicinity.

None of this insisting that there isn't anything to complain about. The most enlightened being is mumbling a harmless complaint to themselves on occasion. The difference is that they are aware of when it happens, and they shift that complaint into a positive action effortlessly. People want to be comfortable and when they feel their comfort is being messed with, then they will complain. Evolving souls prefer to hang around people that complain less over the toxic complainer.

There are different levels of complaining. Some of it is harmless like, "Oh wow it's cold out here I need my jacket."

A toxic complainer is someone that is negatively ranting and raving about on social media or with anyone that will listen to them. They are always complaining about something that they're a drag to be around. It just brings you down.

Day to day issues happen to everyone all around the planet. Some of it can be extreme enough to push you to vent. Even the nicest, sweetest, most compassionate soul complains. This isn't about that, but about being aware and conscious of when you fall into a dark pattern of daily repetitive complaining that it's become all that you are. You know it's an issue when someone you know sees you and they turn the other way to avoid you. Because they know it's going to be the same sad or angry bitter song being played

When you find that you've fallen into perpetual complaining that it's now annoying you, then work on turning that complaint into positive action steps. An action step can be choosing to stop complaining. It can be to look at what you're complaining about and finding creative ways to resolve whatever it is you're complaining about. If it's something that is not realistic or possible to correct, then work on letting it go. Divert your focus towards positive beneficial activities to distract your mind from the negative while adding what you desire to your prayer request.

Positivity Vs. Negativity

You will experience negativity on occasion throughout your life. It's not insisted that you be positive every single second, since that is not realistic or practical for a human being. It is about being mindful and aware of your overall state of mind. This means that as long as you're more positive and optimistic, than negatively stressed, depressed, and angry, then the positive quotient is high enough to pull in positive blessings. You're in the clear if most of the time you're a fairly positive and optimistic person.

When people like you they will say, "He/she is a joy to be around. I just love them."

You know you're in trouble if how they think of you is, "He/she is always complaining about something, I can't stand them."

The dangers of pretending to be positive when deep down you're not is that God and your angels see how you're feeling. You could put on the façade that you're optimistic and positive, but if what you're feeling underneath is struggle and negativity, then that is what is pulled into your life. This is because that is the overall nature you're conveying, not the deceptive friendly face on the exterior, but your soul's entire energetic well-being and state.

Some have said, "I'm not naïve for being positive and optimistic. I just choose to look at the bright side of things."

This is a fantastic mantra to have as long as you're not falling into denial over an abusive situation that's taken place. This is also pending that what you're being optimistic about is aligned with God's will for your soul in the end. Looking to have your ego stroked or having a distorted excited goal of being popular is not aligned with the Light. It's losing your way and falling into the deception of the Darkness.

Deception is not going to be obvious, which is why it's called deception. Deception shows up as something that can easily entice and lure you into its trap. It has to be something or someone attractive enough that it causes you to light up with excitement. This is the danger of deception, because it shows up in this attractive form pulling you in until you later realize that you've been had. "How did I not see this?"

It's because the Darkness shows up in this way. Its goal is to pull you in and drown you in it. You later realize after much time has passed that you got sucked into something that had deceived you. This can apply to anything such as when someone promises you all sorts of stuff that never pans out. You find out you wasted hundreds or thousands of dollars on something pointless that had no positive benefit.

Deception can show up as a hot looking guy or

girl you find attractive. You become blinded by their beauty bending over backwards to cater to their every whim. One day you wake up and realize it was always you being the giver. They were consistently taking advantage of that by receiving and never giving. You obtained a temporary rushed high from the object of your desires positive reaction over what they received from you that you continue to keep giving and giving. That is until you hopefully wake up and realize that there is a grave imbalance in the connection. You could discover they were never truly that interested in you, but couldn't say no to the constant kindness you kept bestowing on them. This is how one gets taken advantage of, which can also lead you to feel resentment.

This is why it's called deception, because deception is not going to show up as deception. It's going to show up as something attractive enough to lure you in and pull you down. It's designed to trick and deceive you into falling for it. When you discover you were deceived, then you look upon it as if you had been out of your mind while the deception took place.

A positive person can fall into despair every now and then, but it is not their permanent daily state. If you're complaining every single day about the same issues for months on end, and there is no positive change, then take a look at that.

There is no doubt that on my journey towards accomplishing what I wanted to, there were moments I ignored my Spirit team's guidance and fell prey to the allure of the Darkness convincing me that I will never obtain what I seek. In younger naïve days, I have been led astray down a different path that looked like it was filled with glitter, but wound up full of deception. I've also fallen into daily complaining about an issue until I received that eye opener. It prompts me to say, "I'm starting to annoy myself. I need to stop this at once. How did I allow this to endure for so long?"

You're suddenly sounding like a broken record at that point, even to yourself.

When you're in tune, aware, and conscious of what's happening around you, then you are also more in tune to picking up on how complaining can make you feel. It doesn't feel good, it lowers your vibration, and you feel this ugly weight on you afterwards. This isn't telling you to never complain as everybody whines on some level. This also isn't saying that there isn't anything to complain about. You could easily find at least one thing to complain about daily.

The moments I'm alone, productive, and working, there are no complaints filtering through my mind. When I'm with a fun positive uplifting friend, there are no complaints moving through either of us, so it is something that can be done. It doesn't even cross our minds. It's only when certain personalities come around that it moves it into a complaint, then I find I've become caught in its web if it continues indefinitely. Find people that tend to move into positivity to connect with.

Generally, it's other people that can infect your aura, specifically the gossipy complaining ones. Sometimes it's just good humor and harmless, but other times it's bathed in hostility. You likely know that one person in your life where every time you bump into them they are harshly complaining about something. If you're a clairsentient sensitive empath type, then you can feel your entire body shift, stress, and tense up. You end up walking away from that person feeling low. When before you encountered them, you were doing great and riding on cloud nine.

There is also that one friend you may know of that every time you bump into them there is some kind of gossip. They see you and shout, "There you are! You are not going to believe what I just found out about Karen."

No one needs to hear about the gossip you've dug up on Karen. Worry about your own life and work on fixing that, because generally if someone's life is that dull they will negatively fixate on other people's lives. The obsession some personality types have for gossip is also what made the tabloid industry a billion-dollar enterprise. They have enough people wanting to follow the lives of the rich and famous to comment on it. Buying tabloids or frequenting gossip sites is not usually to get inspired, but to either falsely worship a celebrity you don't personally know or harshly criticize them. Neither does well to open the floodgates to attracting in abundance and blessings. This is due to the energy involved with gossip and complaining about them.

Everyone complains on some level, which usually comes from the inner feelings experienced. I feel this, I feel that, I feel I feel. Feelings are the culprit for a great deal of unhappiness. It drives one to an addiction. Some complain about their jobs, others complain about the daily traffic, some complain about their friends, family members, lovers or a situation that happened while out at a store.

Become self-aware and mindful of what you're complaining about. Is complaining about it helping to resolve an issue or is it just splattering negative gossip energy around? Notice how you feel when you're complaining as it's happening. It may give some people a rushed high at first, but like sugar or alcohol, you inevitably feel that low drop in energy causing you to crash to the floor. If it's continuously bringing your energy down when you're done venting, then work to detangle from that and let whatever it is bothering you go.

Choose your battles wisely. What situations can use your warrior like vigilance in correcting and what can you foresee as being a complete waste of time. Sometimes it helps to complain about something with someone in order to come to a resolution. You're having relationship issues and don't know what to do about it. When you have the goal of wanting to correct the issue, then complaining can be temporarily warranted. Talking it out with someone can help you come to a resolve that will work. Complaining wanders along that fine line of helpful to toxic. Is the complaining constructive in order to reach a positive resolution? Or is the complaining taking place because you're dying to harshly trash someone because you hate that they're doing well in life while you've been struggling? The latter is non-productive for you since it's not hurting or harming the target, but your own well-being. This is part of taking care of you, so that you can stay on track and on path towards accomplishing your ultimate goals in life. This is whether spiritually, emotionally, mentally, or physically.

Humanity would be a step closer to a Utopian world if everyone would stop ranting and raving about. The repeat offenders don't know to stop and are unable to get over whatever they're constantly angry about. Some of the largest complaining noise happens on social media, which is often used as a public diary to air your venting about what happened when you were trying to get into a parking space at the grocery store.

You likely know there are social media accounts that are filled to the brim of some kind of non-constructive rant about someone or something they despise. This isn't about the occasional slip that an overall positive person falls into where they suddenly take a moment to complain about something. This is about the regular offenders where the majority of their posts are negatively based every hour of every day. It doesn't do anything to help matters. It certainly doesn't contribute to bringing more love into the world. Someone looking to bring more love into the world already knows this won't help their causes.

There are now statistics and scholar studies surrounding the negative effects of social media with sites like Twitter. Twitter has grown to be a platform for predominately negative energy rather than positivity. There is also growing evidence that social media contributes to increasing anxiety and depression symptoms in some people.

There is something eerie about having an unqualified suspect posting something that can negatively destroy someone's well-being by accusing them of a crime they never partook in. This is how dangerous social media has become. Those guilty of it don't feel they're contributing anything negative. When you're buried that deep into it, then it's difficult to see clearly. This is why gossip is considered one of the toxic addictions and part of the deadly sins. This is due to the array of negative issues it causes both to the sender and any recipient. The Darkness wins by using the naïve and guilty as his pawn towards humanities destruction and downfall.

The limitless statistics repeatedly popping up cite and illustrate that many people are finding this to be a growing problem. I also hear from many people informing me they're either distancing themselves or shutting their social media accounts down due to this happening, because it is an epidemic. There are the usual offenders that you know will quickly jump on board with every single daily top trending story that exists. Some of them have hundreds of thousands and millions of followers that bow down to their every word. It's like the pied piper leading them all to slaughter.

There are moments I've fallen into a complaint, but I'm fully aware of it. I've said, "Okay I need to wrap this up and move on, because I'm just irritating myself now."

Dwelling in that kind of toxicity doesn't help anything. Release any anger and resentment you have towards whoever or whatever it is you're complaining about. Let it go because you don't need it. Carrying the pain or heaviness of the complaining energy is not harming the target of your complaint. It is just a toxicity festering inside you that has been scientifically proven to manifest into health issues down the line.

Can you not feel that energy while in the gossip complaint? Are you not tired of living like that? You don't need to carry the unnecessary pain. Give it away to Heaven to transmute and turn it into gold. Pray to be helped from incessant complaints. Ask your Spirit team to help you turn your complaints into positive action.

Do you complain about having no money? What action steps can you do to change that? If the answer is nothing, then that's an action step you're choosing to make. Making no move is making a move.

If your thoughts are filled with negative talk, you may as well work on shifting that to something positive. Since you have thoughts racing in your mind as it is, wouldn't you rather listen to good stuff than bad? No one is forcing you to think a certain way. You have control over what you're thinking. That's one of the things you actually do have control over. You can spend your life regurgitating negative things about yourself, or you can begin the process of adopting more positive things to say about yourself. No one else can control that except you. Look at the good you have now, because you have more good in you than you realize or are willing to admit or notice.

I'm not immune to the occasional negative thoughts and feelings either. It was much more prevalent when I was younger, but as I grew older I learned to stand into my own and appreciate the good aspects of me. It wasn't an overnight change, but a gradual one as I had God and my Spirit team work with me to put this into practice. I don't remember my negative self-talk being particularly severe or damaging. It wasn't as bad as the words my now deceased father said to me growing up that had more of a permanent psychological impact. Ironically, I was particularly loving and supportive towards myself, which no doubt was coming from God.

My motto as a teenager was that if no one will support me, then I will support myself. That still holds true today. By the time I was sixteen, I knew that if I was going to survive on this physical plane that I better find a job. My family was poor, and we grew up with no money, so I knew the only way to not allow that to continue was to fight to make it on my own. I ended up doing that successfully. I prayed, connected to God and my team daily, and followed their action steps. They showed me one thing, I accomplished it, then they showed me another, and I accomplished that, and so on. This is how God works. You'll continuously be shown the same thing for days, weeks, months, and even years until you finally notice the synchronicity to make that move. You delay that move out of fear or by not realizing that it was a psychic hit from

Heaven.

I've heard from others who informed me of their day-to-day negative self-talk that is more along the lines of self-cruelty. Mine was more along the lines of, "Why did I say that to that person?" Or "Now why did I do that?"

I would acknowledge that for a second, but then move on from it and onto other things quickly. It doesn't mean I'm perfection, far from it, but I do my best to be aware and mindful of those moments that any negative feeling or thought I've conjured up isn't real. I realized that most of those feelings and thoughts were ultimately not based in reality, but my own personal human perception.

Imagine spending your days saying sentences like, "I have no talents, I'm not good at anything, no one likes me the way they love others, I'm unlovable, I'm hideous, why would anyone hire me, why would anyone want to be with me, I'm useless, I can't do anything right, I'll never amount to anything, I have nothing to be grateful for, my life sucks, it's always one thing after another going wrong, I'm too young, I'm too old, I'm too fat, I'm too thin…."

That must have annoyed or brought you down to read. As an ever-inquisitive bee having communicated with so many people over the years I've discovered that everyone has those negative thoughts about themselves to one extent or another. For some it only enters their mind once in awhile, and for others it's a constant daily attack of badgering of themselves. Their perception of themselves is negatively skewed.

Where can it get you to sit around all day thinking low thoughts one after the other?

Love yourself because you are created in His image. You were born out of love from the creator who loves you unconditionally. Those negative words you tell yourself are untrue lies fed to you by the devil's darkness. They seem or feel true from your own current reality and perception, but not in the eyes of God. Not in the eyes of those in Heaven. Your soul is perfection in every way and loved unconditionally for all that you are, including your strengths and what you consider to be personal flaws. Love, accept, and appreciate you, because you're a gift!

CHAPTER EIGHT

Taking Action
on Divine Guidance

You've done the visualization exercises, the dream boards, prayed and asked for help, yet nothing has moved in your life or has been forthcoming. Take a step back for a moment and look at any repetitive ideas that may have continuously entered your mind urging you to take action on. What repetitive feelings or thoughts have been hitting you, but you've brushed it aside, ignored it, or not followed it. This process requires your intuitive powers to determine whether the action step you keep getting is one generated from your ego or is divinely guided.

Generally, a divinely guided idea or action step will come into your consciousness several times or more, whereas something from your ego may come in an inconsistent way. A Divine impression that sifts into your soul would be an idea that harms no one including yourself on any level whether emotionally, physically, mentally or spiritually.

Ideas that are manufactured from the ego would be things like get rich quick schemes or a longing for public notoriety, popularity, or fame. Fame is usually just a side effect that happens out of one's talent or gifts, but it's not something the talented person seeks out. They just want to be able to participate in work they love. Any fame or fortune that enters the picture is a side effect of diving into that passion, but it is one that the talented person could do without as long as they can do their work without fear of not having enough money to pay their bills.

Your Spirit team steps in to assist you while on your journey. They guide you towards particular accomplishments at the right time. They could be helping you with a specific issue indefinitely for awhile, but then there are times where they step back and allow you to make a free will choice. They can't live your life for you and make every single shred of decision making. You would never learn anything or experience life if they were continuously making all of your choices for you. Since most people don't typically listen to other people, it's unlikely they would listen to their Spirit team.

Your Spirit team may guide you by getting you to notice someone or something that can help you achieve a particular desire. It could be by implanting the information into your consciousness where you can sense you're supposed to take action on something. They will continue to offer the same action step indefinitely until you finally take it. It doesn't matter if one week passes or one year. That same action step will be put in front of you until it's taken. Once you've taken action on that step, then they will show you the next step and so forth.

When it comes to matters of love, they will put particular soul mate choices in your path intended to connect with you, but then it is up to you and/or this other person to notice it and act on it. They work with the other person's guides to guide that person toward you, while your own guides are guiding you towards them. That's quite a bit of guiding going on behind the scenes in hopes that both parties notice. They'll get you in the room alone together to face each other, but then it's up to the both of you to do the rest of the work. If neither of you do, then it's back to the drawing board for both sets of guides to continuously work to orchestrate the meeting again and again in hopes that action will be taken. This can only go on for so long before the moment passes, and neither is unable to keep the orchestration from happening. At that point a lost opportunity has passed for both parties.

Perhaps you are afraid about taking that divinely guided step, or you don't know how you'll do it, or you've already tried that, but it didn't work. The idea is still coming in trying to get you to notice it for a reason. Don't discredit those divinely guided ideas that require you to take action. Taking action is another key step to opening the floodgates of abundance and blessings in your life.

Act on the continuing positive nudges you receive and follow it. Don't allow worry or fear to set in blocking you from moving forward. Avoid inviting in more of that negative worry stuff to you. Some people choose to create a vision board, images, or positive words posted around them that remind them of what they want. This assists in implanting the ideas into your mind, which will help direct the energy towards making something happen. The goal is to fill your life with positive words and phrases that are aligned with abundance.

Affirm only what you desire and not what is lacking or missing in your life. The more you affirm what you don't want, then the more likely you will bring in that which you don't want into your life. Since that's the case, you may as well work on affirming positive thoughts and feelings. It's easy to live in negativity since that's what the Darkness drives each soul to reside in. No one is exempt from the ego taking over and talking you out of positivity.

If you perpetually keep displaying negative thoughts and feelings, then changing that process will take daily practice to re-train your mind to think differently. Don't feel discouraged if you find that you keep reverting back to negativity or that it becomes difficult. Notice when the negativity comes in, pay attention to when that happens, and shift the energy into positive thoughts and feelings. It also helps to work with a close friend where you can both catch each other when taking things too far into negativity for too long. At the same time that doesn't mean to pretend you're fine when you're not feeling it. It takes a great deal of work to lift your vibration out of the doldrums and upwards into God's light. It may take you months as you implement this new mindset into more optimism than pessimism. Practice altering your thoughts and feelings to positive ones. Being mindful and aware of when you fall into a negative pattern can help accomplish this.

Pray Instead of Worry

Challenges can be easier to move through when you pray and ask for daily help and guidance. This must also be followed up with you paying attention to the repetitive guidance coming in, then you take action on that guidance. Often when you ask for help in prayer you will be guided to take action on something to help it along. Pay attention to the recurring guidance asking you to take action on something. It will continue to come into your aura indefinitely until you do it. This taking action step will never ask you to harm, hurt, or hate anyone including yourself.

Prayer is intended to help you move away from worry and fear. You invalidate a prayer when you continue to worry afterwards. The worry tells Spirit that you don't trust their intervention and assistance and so you will continue to worry as a backup plan in case God doesn't come through. When you receive repeated nudges after the prayer to take action on something, then take action.

Worry is a negative based emotion that makes you believe that something is not going to go according to plan. Sometimes that can create a self-fulfilling prophecy and push what you desire further away from you. You want to ensure that your thoughts and feelings remain positive that you will obtain what you desire.

Most don't favor constant change as it disrupts the momentum they've become comfortable in. All human beings are equal in the end regardless of what they look like, where they are from, or what lifestyle choices they make. No one is better than anyone else even though each of the ego's attempts to scream the loudest to let others know their way and opinion is the best route. In the end, all the world hears is noise. There is no Divine energy light that exists anywhere within that noise.

Others choose not to believe in a higher power when their prayers have gone unanswered. I've had my own share of roadblocks, but there are numerous unseen reasons as to why prayers go unanswered. When it's a human souls time to pass on, praying can alleviate any hardship for that soul crossing over, but it won't necessarily stop them from passing on, because eventually souls will pass on. That soul might have agreed to pass on during that time in that way for a lesson they chose to learn.

There are various reasons that Heavenly requests are not always fulfilled. Sometimes what you're requesting isn't aligned with your higher self and may cause unseen harm or turmoil. Other times there are pieces to the puzzle that need to be adjusted before something can come to fruition. They may also have something better in mind that you're not seeing. One of the other reasons is you're being guided to take specific action steps to help something come along, but you're not pursuing it. Follow the repetitive guidance and messages you're receiving by taking action with the steps you're given.

You're wrestling with an issue, so you request heavenly intervention and assistance mentally or out loud in a prayer. It feels rushed or forced and your ego gets in the way convincing you that no one can understand or hear you from above. You are heard regardless of your state of being at that moment and whether or not you believe your request for help sounds messed up or garbled. With intention simply saying, "Heaven help!" has already formed the connection.

Observe humility, appreciation, and gratitude. When you experience testy times, it doesn't help when your focus is on the drama swirling around you. When you shift that energy into something positive, then the drama grows less hostile as your higher self rises back up and takes charge. Your higher self is the part of your soul that is the most connected to God.

Be appreciative for the good you have in your life now. This is shifting negative complaining words and thoughts into something positive. What you're thinking and feeling now is what dictates the direction of how your life will go in the coming months. Sometimes you can get caught up in what you don't have instead of the good that you do have.

It's easy to get caught up in the good that comes in. This is where you ignore where these blessings are coming from. The feeling behind being grateful is a high vibration energy, which attracts in more of the same. Gratitude goes a long way towards manifesting higher soul feeling experiences.

Pay Attention to Divine Guidance

Maybe an action step you're guided to make is taking you out of your comfort zone. You're afraid of making a drastic move that you know deep down you desperately want to make, but you're fearful of what will or will not come if you take action. Trust the continuous guidance your Spirit team is giving you. This is putting your faith and trust in God and the Universe that there is a Divine plan laid out to assist you. You will never be guided into something that God doesn't think you can handle.

You want to be realistic and practical while making Earthly decisions, such as you want to be careful walking away from a job when you don't have another one lined up. There are a great many success stories that include someone taking a huge risk by walking away from a job before they found another. Still you want to move cautiously with that kind of a major decision.

A reader named John owns an art gallery selling

expensive art to high end clients. Before he was doing that, he was a salesperson for a company. He would work from home most of the time, but wasn't putting in much of an effort as a salesperson. His heart wasn't in it, so instead he dabbled around with this art selling idea. Eventually the company he was a salesperson at let him go when they discovered he wasn't putting in any effort. After he was let go he dove head on into his work as an art dealer. He opened his gallery and ended up attracting in all sorts of clients and buyers that his side business started booming. He now owns this successful business. He was also able to buy his own home and he's never been happier.

The way he told me the story had struck a positive inspirational chord, as I've listened to other similar stories. Sometimes getting fired, laid off, or quitting is the severe push one needs to completely focus on their side business and making it a full-time money-making business. It's true that it can be risky doing it that way, but many have been successful at that. They're no longer being weighed down by this day job that drops their vibration making them miserable. That state is not helpful in building your side business.

When they were let go from the day job, this put them into high gear where they kicked up the action efforts into their side business. They had a bit of a financial cushion to give themselves a few months to dive into building this side business without fear of not being able to pay their bills. In John's case, he was able to increase the income as an art dealer to the point that looking for another day job was no longer necessary. This isn't advising you to quit your job if that's a concern. Always move cautiously with big decisions weighing the pros and cons before acting. When in doubt revert to prayer for guidance.

Maybe your Spirit team continues to nudge you to apply for a job you always wanted, but you had already applied at that same place a year prior and received no response. Months or a year later the job is still on your mind. Many companies are open to people re-applying or re-submitting their resume or credentials every six months. You may have received no response the first time, but the repetitive Spirit guidance coming in on it again may be no accident. You're being asked to try again, as they see the timing is now right. Your name also becomes more familiar to the employer that does the hiring. They are more likely to call a familiar name to come in for an interview over a name they don't know.

This same scenario has been true for me. As far as with the jobs I've had in the past from the record store to the film business. I was turned down initially or I received no response from them. I tried on numerous occasions on a later date and received no response or they'd say something like, "Sorry we're not hiring right now".

I tried again at a much later date and that was when I struck gold. This time I received a response to come in, met with them, and was hired on the spot. Imagine if I didn't follow the hunches to try again.

Perhaps you were turned down or you turned them down, but the hunches kept coming in stronger over time, so you try again. It's the trying again part in the equation when it all comes together.

Sometimes you're supposed to be at a specific job at a time in your life for a reason that might not be understood while it's in motion. You may be longing to quit this day job for some time and cannot understand what the delay is. You could be gaining skills at this day job that you will be utilizing later. You may not think so at the time you are working the job. It's only in the future when you're at the next gig or chapter in your life that you look back and realize why you were there for the time that you were. This concept goes for relationships of all types from friendships, business, to love as well too.

You could be single and constantly bumping into the same person in passing or while out and about getting you both to notice one another. You and this person may secretly be developing a crush on one another that you start to pick up on with the mutual warm smiles and hello-how are you's. As time progresses you both gain confidence to say more than hello and strike up longer conversations. This is how I've met some of the ones I ended up with in long term love relationships with in the past.

There are times where you've been psychically blocked or you're not receiving a crystal-clear Divine answer on something, while other times it will slam into your consciousness in a matter of seconds. For those times where nothing is coming in, it helps to pray, connect with God, ask for intervention, signs, messages, and guidance. Ask your Spirit team to help you notice what these messages could be.

Before bed and drifting off to sleep, ask your Spirit team to come into your dreams and communicate with you there. Your ego is asleep, and your consciousness rises leaving you more receptive and open to receiving the Divine content while in a dream state. Ask that they help you remember the dream, because sometimes the dreams can be so vivid, but the second you wake up it's gone and vanished. Keep a journal or notepad within reach while asleep so that when you wake up, you can quickly jot down the images you received in the dream as soon as possible before it's gone. Even if it has no meaning to you at that point. Jot it down as it could have significance later.

Dreaming is also connected to Clairvoyance, which is clear psychic seeing or clear viewing. Many that have vivid dreams regularly tend to have strong Clairvoyance. Clairvoyance requires some decoding on your part, since the messages come in as visuals that are more symbolic than a direct message. Write down everything you remember seeing in the dream, even if it was a color. Colors have symbolic meanings as well too. There could be some important clues in your dreams that were planted into your subconscious from Heaven to help you.

CHAPTER NINE

Gratitude and Optimism

Gratitude is one of the greater ways to increase bounty in your life. This is not fake appreciation with the hidden goal of obtaining increase, since Heaven knows when you're being deceptive. It has to be a genuine gratitude where you truly do feel this gratitude within every cell of your being. Gratitude is a challenging trait to display because the darkness of ego part of someone desires to be thankless preferring to be greedy. In America, on Thanksgiving the tradition is everyone gives thanks and gratitude to those around them. The irony is the next day is Black Friday, one of the larger shopping days of the year causing a rise in greed and violence. If you do an internet search of, "Black Friday greed" or "Black

Friday violence", then no additional proof or validation of this greed is required. You'll find endless pages of it.

Be grateful for what you have in your life here and now. Living in a miserable or pessimistic state blocks the flow of abundance and increases the challenges in your life due to God's law of the universe.

You could be struggling in life and facing insurmountable challenges, but everyone is battling something. Some of those challenges they're battling with could be considered as being worse than someone else's depending on whom you ask. Any form of uncomfortable struggle still counts as energy in the eyes of the Universe.

This isn't telling you not to fall into pessimism or negativity, because everyone has some measure of struggle. Even the most optimistic person will experience some browbeaten feelings and thoughts. No one is exempt from challenges. This is just explaining what can block the flow of positive abundance, blessings, and answered prayers.

All energy expands regardless of the tone of that energy. If you're positive, then this positive energy will expand. If it's negative, then that's what will expand and bring more of that to you. Since this is deemed the case, functioning in an optimistic state when it is possible will have more benefit than not.

Don't force positivity if you're not feeling it. Avoid beating yourself up if you're battling negatively. Take your time being aware of the moments you're in a negative state. Look at what is causing it, then examine what action steps you can take to relieve that stress. If you are unable to do anything about it, then work on letting it go.

You could be sitting in daily traffic that doesn't move, which always angers and upsets you. Sitting in your car in upset will not lighten the traffic. It also won't help in getting to your destination quicker. All it does is attack your soul and pull you down. You arrive at your location stressed and edgy. When you look at the detrimental effects it places on your back, then it's easier to move out of that.

Mentally say in prayer, *"I don't want to live in misery. I need to shake this off. God please help me move out of this stress and back into joy."*

When I've been in those situations I've worked extra hard to move my angry stressed thoughts into something more productive. Use that time to mentally communicate to God and your Spirit team to help alleviate the stress you continue to feel over circumstances you cannot do anything about. In addition, ask for Divine help in mending the areas that you are able to. Ask God for help and to put ideas in your mind that you can take action on to fix a situation you'd like to see positive changes with.

It can be easy to fall into a state of pessimism when nothing good is going for you, but if you're breathing and you're alive, then that's something to be grateful for. Do you have a place to lay your head, food on the table, clothing, and the basic practical survival necessities needed? Then that's something to be grateful for. Imagine having one or all of that taken away with no one to turn to, because this has happened to a great number of people all across history. How would you feel if that happened?

Statistics have revealed that more people than not despise their job. Many people rightly complain about their job, especially if you're working in an abusive environment with toxic people. It could be a soul crushing job that kills off your life force. You could work with one or more difficult people. You partake in work that doesn't inspire you to want to do it, but you do it for the paycheck to survive. You're not partaking in work that you're passionate about. When you move back into gratitude, you're able to observe the job from a higher perspective. The more challenging plight is when the job is toxic or abusive. Pray daily for a way out into something better and more improved.

Otherwise say in prayer, *"I know I sometimes complain about my job, and I do want to make a positive job change, but at the same time I am grateful that I have a paycheck coming in. I know if I didn't have that, then who knows what would happen. In that respect, I am grateful for this job. I'll do my best to look at it positively while I'm there until I can find another change I can make to move out of that."*

State that kind of a positive prayer affirmation by not just saying the words, but realize how the words ring true. Feel the gratitude that you have this job and are genuinely blessed. Through move you are raising your vibration again. The vibration is being raised to match the level of the type of blessings you wish to attract into your life. You are the magnet and the abundance is the steel. You are drawing it towards or away from you depending on your actions, thoughts, and feelings of every moment of every day.

Heaven and the Universe, which we use interchangeably, ensure your basic needs are met. They help with what you need, not always necessarily with what you want, especially if what you want is not beneficial for your higher self. If they do see that it will benefit your growth and higher self, then they will work with you to help bring that which you desire to fruition. All potential and possible factors would need to be examined for each person.

There are various time delays per person as to when particular blessings are bestowed on that soul. Each person's trajectory is different from another person's. It's not that one person is more worthy of blessings over another soul. There are various factors that have to come into play as to what is delaying blessings and miracles.

For every soul on Earth, the desire for blessings and miracles have many factors which come into play to determine whether they will be granted. For someone in the United States, they may have a middle class somewhat comfortable lifestyle as opposed to someone born in a country or area where restrictions, suffocation, bondage, and resistance are evident. There are third world countries where people live in inadequate and unsafe conditions. They may never know what it's like to be able to manifest what they desire.

At the same time, many are brought up in these conditions where they know no other way. They may not have television or internet and have no idea of what is happening in other parts of the world. They may be perfectly content because it is all they know. They weren't brought up in a country or city that displays a desire for excess in front of them around the clock. What they choose to desire may not be as high as what someone else desires in a wealthier city.

The person in a Third World Country may desire to attract in enough food for one night's dinner. Whereas in another part of the world, that wealthy person is bombarded with imagery that you can be whatever you want to be and achieve whatever you want to achieve if you set your mind to it. Maybe you will, but will that bring you ultimate happiness?

Ultimate happiness is the state of high personal soul power. It's climbing beyond the superficiality and the physical to achieve an absolute transcending spiritual life force that is perfectly aligned with God.

The positive side effect to that utopia reached is additional physical manifestations, blessings, and abundance flowing in. Many that reach a higher soul spiritual level no longer desire materialistic excess. This is not limited to the basic human survival needs of a home, food, and clothing. Add to that good friends or a loyal loving love partner, pending you desire the latter. Some spiritual soul achievers tend to be perfectly comfortable alone.

Sometimes it can be that you are indeed ready

for blessings. You've done the hard work and experienced what you were intended to in order to bring you to the place you're at today. You have consistently maintained this hard work ethic, but still nothing has transpired to help you have that breakthrough you've long desired. You've done everything right, but nothing has come to pass. In those cases, there are other elements at play preventing the blessings from coming in.

It can be your Spirit team is working diligently behind the scenes with you, but there are free will choice delays that have taken place. It can be that those who are intended to notice your hard work are not paying attention to it, even though the signs have been in front of them forever. Other times it can be that you're doing everything right, but you express no gratitude. Complaining and worry just tells the universe bring me this thing I don't want as fast as you can. All it does is reverse the positive manifestation process into negative manifestation.

Work on being grateful for what you have now. Being ungrateful will block and delay what you desire. It's that negative energy that stalls forward movement. It's understandable to feel frustrated when you've been doing the hard work for so long and yet nothing has come to assist and give you that big miracle breakthrough you long for. It's not like you're being punished, and that God is purposely withholding blessings from you while granting it to others that you feel are less deserving of it. Feeling envy blocks the flow of abundance. It's also not anyone's place to decide who is worthy of what and when. There are varying time limits for each person that determine when and if abundance will flow in and what that will entail.

You're going to feel negative feelings on occasion in terms of what is or isn't coming in. You'll feel frustrated and envious of others that seem to get blessed instantly. This is about recognizing when those feelings hit you and working quickly to eradicate it and move back into a positive alignment. It takes practice and discipline to re-train your mind into a new way of thinking and seeing things. Changing your ways will not drastically happen overnight. It's a gradual methodical process that will take work and focus on your part.

Whenever you notice anything good happening in your life, whether or not it's big or small, remember to say daily, "I Am Blessed!"

You are blessed in the smallest of details, the smallest of ways, there is that glimmer of light that attempts to crack its way in to help you remember to believe again. If you're interested in attracting in positive circumstances, then be genuinely grateful in prayer for what you have now.

CHAPTER TEN

Grieving, Depression, Suicide

Perhaps you are battling with emotional or mental challenges. You reside in a cutthroat ego dominating world that has the attitude of kill or be killed. This hyper technological age has diminished face to face interaction and trained others to conduct themselves like cold aloof robots. The more sensitive souls struggle to stay afloat while battling a consistent array of depression or anxiety symptoms in the mix of this warzone.

There is a difference between being born into this life with a brain chemistry imbalance to feeling the occasional depression blues. Depression blues that hit you once in a rare while can be triggered by poor lifestyle choices or a negative circumstance that knocks you off cloud nine. Those that experience the rare blues usually bounce back if their innate personality is typically upbeat and optimistic. There are those that have always suffered from depression and anxiety symptoms their entire Earthly life.

Depression and anxiety symptoms that develop and remain within the composites of your soul in this lifetime don't have to be seen as a curse. Some of it is connected to your sensitivities, which are connected to your Clairsentience psychic clair channel, which can be channeled positively through artistic and creative pursuits.

Your sensitivities are a gift from Heaven to use towards the self-improvement of your soul as well as the betterment of humanity. Many with heightened sensitivity and stimuli have been able to turn their sensitivities into a successful career in the creative world. They are the artists of the world, such as actors, entertainers, painters, singers, writers, photographers and the list goes on. When they channel their sensitivities positively, there is no telling what they can accomplish. Unfortunately, the downside is when they're unable to channel it positively or they vacillate back and forth from channeling it positively and producing striking work to falling into the darkness of depression symptoms. Some depression symptoms are terribly severe that it leads that human soul to suicidal thoughts.

If you battle with emotional and mental issues in this lifetime such as depression and anxiety, know that you are more psychically in tune than you realize. There is assistance out there in finding healthful ways to temper it or control the onslaught of depression emotions experienced.

Many well-known artists such as actors and singers have resorted to suicide which has devastated the world prompting a discussion in many circles to take depression and suicide seriously. On the flipside, there are the negative critics popping in that are lucky enough to be cruising through life as happy campers. They've made erroneous statements such as suicide being a selfish act or that if you're depressed to get over it. These people are disconnected from their soul consciousness and anything outside of their physical body. They have been blessed enough to be removed from the imbalances created in more sensitive beings due to the harshness of the Earth's environment.

I'm often asked how is it that a person's guides and angels don't stop something like suicide from happening. This is asked as if Heaven isn't doing anything on their end to stop it. They're merely sitting around twiddling their thumbs. Human souls have free will choice in order to learn and grow their soul. Free will choice means that no heavenly being can intervene without the person's expressed permission. That means if the person is feeling suicidal, then a simple prayer and call out to God can help get the ball rolling.

Where suicide is concerned, the soul's guide and angel are doing what they can to ease that soul's heart and convince them not to do something that will prove fatal. However, as many sensitive beings understand, when you're experiencing negative emotions such as depression, anger, fear or upset, then you're not picking up on anything outside of yourself, let alone your own Spirit team's communications from Heaven. You're only hearing the shouting negativity of your own thoughts which spreads in your mind like a poison.

It isn't uncommon for artists of all types to suffer from depression. They are highly tuned in psychic sensitive sponges able to walk in someone else's shoes. They hold the least amount of judgment by being able to look at a cruel person and find that person's heart when playing a character. Having grown up and worked in the entertainment business, I see them as just like everybody else. They have immense success and talent, but they are struggling with more internal issues and demons beyond the public's comprehension.

A great deal of human souls born into this lifetime and those beyond are ultra-sensitive. They've been planted on Earth or we should say plopped in the middle of a battlefield. Hostile and barbaric human souls surround the sensitives in this world. They tamper and wreak harsh energy that causes long term side effects on the more evolved and evolving souls.

Someone that was bullied growing up by other kids will choose to turn the dark into something light. They'll make light of the darkness by making jokes about it and everything else. For some this might not be enough if the internal turmoil goes untreated. Others resort to drugs and alcohol to quiet the inner demons and to feel happy if just for five minutes. The physical life at times becomes too overbearing on souls battling with ongoing depression.

One's life rarely stays the same and circumstances are always changing. Although it can be tough navigating through life's pitfalls and challenges, you do not have to do it all alone. Prayer is one of the greater ways to help temper all of this as much as possible. You can pray for healing or to be led to help calm any depression and anxiety down. You can pray to be guided to the right Doctor, Counselor, or Healer that can take care of you through the right professional medical care. There is nothing off limits when it comes to prayer, even if you're praying for world domination. This doesn't mean a prayer like that will be answered, but the point is there are no exemptions on the list of things to pray for. This is one of the greatest things God has given and that is a direct line to Him and your Spirit team 24/7 free of charge.

The doorway of communication to Heaven is always open to speak as freely as you choose, and you will never be judged. How awesome is that to actually be able to say whatever you like to them and there is no risk of being judged, attacked, or harshly critiqued the way you would be on this Hell on Earth by other people?

Call on your heavenly team of guides and angels who are on standby to partner up with you in order to make some of these challenges in your life more manageable.

It's important to take depression seriously and

get the treatment necessary to continue on. It's also important to remember the body of work that one has donated for the improvement of humanity. This is what will remain alive in years to come, rather than the matter of how one's soul moved into the next plane.

There are sometimes many violent ways in which a soul's life might end in its lifetime. When someone takes their own life via free will or due to a chemical imbalance with their mental health state, then they do so before their time. When this happens, their soul goes into a state of shock as it crosses over. The state that you're in upon suicide as you cross over could stay relatively the same for some. If you had a large ego, then that large ego is still intact as you're crossing over.

If you were suffering from depression and you took your own life, then the state you were in when you took your own life is still present as your soul is crossing over. It's not a pleasant way to cross over because you took your life for the hope of release, but you're not released long after your soul has been extricated from your temporary body. There is a process that takes place in restoring that soul to full capacity. There's a delay before that happens. Sometimes the soul that took their life is disoriented. At the same time there is no pain when crossing over. Any pain that exists is only when in the physical human body. If a soul committed suicide, then like any soul crossing over there are angels and guides surrounding that soul to usher them through the difficulties it might be having.

There are other things that the soul agreed upon as well when they entered this life. If they take their life prematurely, then many end up having to incarnate into another human body and go through similar issues and circumstances all over again. Therefore, it's only bad from the perspective of that soul. It's not bad in the way others preach how you're not supposed to take your own life, or you go to Hell. It's that you had a contract agreed upon to fulfill. If nothing is fulfilled, then it just gets added to a new contract.

Grieving

Human life is accustomed to losses that cause a heavy dark cloud over one's heart. Losses include the human death of someone close to you or the loss of a deep love relationship that ended. Any loss that causes prolonged grief is included. From the perspective of spirit, there is no real loss in this scenario. These losses are part of the human soul experience, but this is an illusion. They do not exist in the bigger reality of why you are here.

Everything you have ever loved or missed comes back to you when your Earthly class is complete. Those grieving over the human death of a loved one must understand that it is not a death in the way that you know it. That soul simply graduated from their Earthly class life run. The uncomfortable heavy weight of the human vessel they occupied was shed off of them. They soared effortlessly into the next room where you will one day re-unite with them. The transition for most is incredibly smooth! There is no pain since pain exists in the Earth's atmosphere. This Earthly life school is equated to boot camp for the soul!

The exceptions are the souls that reside in negative dark energy that have enacted hatred and violence on others. They endure a different process than other souls do, which often requires being diverted into the back gate or left door, which is not a door any soul should desire to go in.

The feeling of grief where you have lost someone you deeply cherished and loved can be challenging to overcome. It is more that you are afraid of the unknown or not seeing concrete proof that your loved one is still around. The ego mind that is detached from spirit conjures up all sorts of conclusions of the worst possible scenarios that there is no next life. As a human soul, it is a process of adjustment when the one you love is not in front of you. It doesn't mean that they're gone in the reality sense. You will be seeing your loved ones again when your Earthly run is complete. All that you loved and lost will be present when your class here is over. As your grieving dissolves you grow more in tune to your surroundings. Grief blocks heavenly communication and you're unable to notice when the loved one is communicating with you from the Other Side. Over time as you raise your vibration from grief, you'll notice the signs and ways your departed loved one is saying 'hello' or communicating with you in the interim.

Often times when a human soul is grieving over the passing of a departed loved one, it pulls the departed soul back into the Earth plane. When you make peace with the one that has passed on, then you release the grieving attachment to them that might keep the soul stuck in this plane. See the soul as exiting through an etheric doorway of heavenly light where they will be doing fantastic! You will see your departed loved one again when your lifetime is complete. In the meantime, they will be with you, watching you, and working with you as one of your guides from time to time. They will be there to greet you when you enter that doorway of light yourself.

When feeling the heaviness of grief, revert to prayer to help you cope and continue on. Ask in prayer that signs of their soul's existence be shown to you. And as always seek out professionals such as grief counselors, support groups, and friendships and family members you trust to be rejuvenated to continue on knowing your loved one is still with you and helping you heal.

CHAPTER ELEVEN

The Significance of Spirituality

There have been numerous polls over the years showing that more people identify as "Spiritual, but not religious" as opposed to those that identify as atheist or strictly religious and not spiritual. This is one way that the repetitive scientific data is indicating that there truly has been a rise in spiritual interests since the 1980's. It accelerated post 2000 as we moved more into the technological era with social media. This is one of the positives of the Internet, technology, and social media.

Part of these findings may be due to how easily information is accessed now online. Before that time period, many people secretly wanted to be more spiritual, but feared ridicule so they went along with pretending to be a hardcore religious person when in the company of other religious people. They didn't have access to communities that had a similar mindset before the Internet domination. Some of the content I talked about during that time was that people were moving away from the fundamentalist religious belief systems and atheism, while becoming more spiritual. We're now seeing these findings to be true.

Without people knowing what I do upon first meeting they would be talking about God and faith, but then would quickly say, "I'm spiritual but not religious." They're saying that to inform the other person not to worry they're not judgmental and full of hate and condemnation the way one expects a religious person to be. Saying that you're spiritual but not religious shows someone has a strong faith-based belief system, but without all of the hate filled dogma that one would associate with a fundamentalist preacher.

Because of this rising spiritual but not religious mindset that has grown astronomically post 2000's, some churches have begun to adopt more lenient policies to welcome more patrons since they started to simultaneously witness a decline in fellowship. This is especially the case for gays who face so much hatred, wrath, and condemnation from some people. All of this because they cannot but be attracted to someone of the same gender. It was how God made them, but they are faced with backlash over it. I've heard of many churches that have become more welcoming for gays, which naturally has also drawn ire from the more fundamentalist patrons. The greatest irony is the fundamentalists go to a house of worship to be taught to remember God's top mantra of love, but are unable to extend that love to all people from all walks of life.

Spirituality is asking the bigger questions and being open to the understanding that there is much more to an Earthly life than the physical material world of narcissism created by human ego. Someone can consider themselves spiritual if they are religious and go to Church regularly. They can also be someone who enjoys going to New Age stores, playing with Tarot cards, or reading self-help books. The spiritual person can be someone that is solely interested in improving one's well-being and subsequently the way they live and their quality of life. The list is long as to how deep the spirituality genre can go and what that individual soul identifies it to be for them.

Someone that considers themselves to be a spiritual person will more than likely be curious, interested, or at least open to all facets of the genre. This is one who is interested in deeper philosophical knowledge as to why they are here or how everything was created. They want to know how to improve themselves and this world. Their belief in God will vary from believing in some form of higher power to not believing in any type of God, Light, or spirit. They might follow and enjoy all facets of spirituality, but will not believe there is any kind of God. God also has different meanings for people depending on who you talk to.

A spiritual person that does not believe in any kind of God is not to be confused with an atheist who tends to not believe in anything, except that when you die you're done and all goes black, the end. An atheist does not believe in God, an afterlife, or any form of metaphysics, spirituality, new age, religion, or God. Even though they might lump the entire spiritual genre together, generally they take issue with organized religion, God, the Bible, and religious dogma. They find the mere mention of an afterlife to be hogwash, and any hint of spirituality to be New Age phooey. An agnostic is someone more open minded to the possibility of some form of God or afterlife, but they do not fully believe in it, yet they also do not fully believe that there is nothing after this either. They hang in the middle requiring physical evidence to convince them. They're more likely to be open to spiritual pursuits in order to assist them on their quest for this knowledge.

I've witnessed atheists transitioning into having more of an open mind when they get their toes wet in any level of spirituality that they feel some form of comfort with. They receive a big enough jolt in their life that leads them to begin questioning and thus becoming more of a spiritual person or agnostic. There are atheists who might not believe in any of it, but are still drawn to spiritual or self-improvement books and interests. In a sense, they're not realizing at that moment they're moving from atheist into an agnostic. Many tend to use labels on themselves that they don't truly understand the meaning of. All human souls are spiritual beings regardless if they believe in that or not.

Earth and all of the planets came from

somewhere. They did not suddenly appear in a perfectly orchestrated solar system that affects the energies in humankind depending on its planetary path. An explosion did not create a setup of planets that circle the Sun in a flawlessly designed fashion and then permanently stayed that way. Pluto is the only planet farthest from the Sun to be detected by humankind. This does not mean there are no other planets or galaxies beyond that, as there most definitely are. Humankind is just unable to detect that. No other life form outside of Earth has been detected scientifically after eons of centuries gone by. As big as the universe is, all life forms seemingly only inhabit Earth, or so one believes.

Almost eight billion people on Earth in this solar system at this time in Earth's history are not an accident. This also gives you some perspective as to how miniscule humankind is in the grand scheme of things. You venture off into space to planet Jupiter or Neptune, then suddenly life on Earth appears immensely ridiculous and trivial from that distance. All of the fighting, disagreeing, pollution, harm, and negative words darted back and forth to one another make humankind look rather silly. You can get a pretty good idea as to how Heaven views the planet from where they are. All of the nonsense that goes on means nothing to them. They watch everyone hate, hurt, and harm one another and roll their eyes with indifference so to speak.

Others find it difficult to believe that God, the archangels, and the angels are unaffected by the harm people are doing to one another. This is thinking from the ego and in a limited way. God, the archangels, and the angels are egoless, which means they have no ego. When you have no ego, then you're unaffected by anything. It does not mean that you do not care, but you are not ruffled emotionally. An egoless being witnesses harmful destruction and feels nothing. You have a detached perception. You view things from a higher perspective. This is not to be confused with a murdering terrorist or serial killer who is without a conscious. They have a dark ego that governs their life demanding they kill. They want control, which is an ego trait.

When you're upset, then this is your ego. God, the archangels, and angels do not get upset because they are egoless. Someone might say operating from ego, "God will punish you for that." This is that person's projection of hoping that God will punish that person, but God does not chastise.

There are ego beings in Heaven, but their ego is not out of control the way it would be in the Earth's atmosphere living a human life. Go back through centuries of history to the beginning of Earth's conception and the start of humankind. At least one man and one woman would have needed to be present in order to multiply. It is not by chance that they were suddenly here and figured out how to mate. They did not evolve out of apes and then stopped evolving out of them. They did not rise from the dirt and appear. There are circumstances existing that are larger than the human mind can comprehend. Science has attempted to make sense of it all, but without much luck enough to convince every person. This is going back to the initial creation of life, the planets, people, animals, plants came together in ways that a non-believer wouldn't be able to fathom or comprehend. There is no data that exists of when the first man walked the Earth and what that was like. There was no language or concept of anything being what already is. The spiritual connections were stronger at the dawn of humankind because there were limited distractions and blocks that the darkness of ego would later create within them.

It was human instinct to connect sexually and suddenly people were being born and multiplying at a rapid rate out of that. They soon believed that it was God's purpose for them to continuously procreate. Breeding intelligently is one thing, but multiplying to eight billion people shows that most reproduce out of ignorance, naivety, and to fulfill ego desires. Earth is a rapid ant farm with people screaming and starving for attention, power, and domination. If this increases it will have catastrophic consequences.

Every living soul is a descendant of the first man that walked the Earth. No one is separated by color, culture, or any other factor. The darkness of ego caused separation from one another. When someone is not evolving, then they view their surroundings and other souls in a limited way. They are uncomfortable with anyone that identifies as different from them being in their vicinity. The ego will grow angry and cause them harm, hurt, or hate just because the other person is not an identical clone. The ego sees this person as threatening, instead of viewing others with understanding, love, acceptance, and compassion.

You move into the realms of spirituality when you start asking the bigger questions such as, "Why am I here?" and "Why are some people different?" or "Is Heaven Real?" You understand there is much more to life than the mundane physical existence that has been structured and set up by human beings of years past. As a spiritual person you have a belief in a higher power, energy, light, spirit or life force. You have a belief that when your life run is complete that it is not the end. Someone spiritual has their own personal barometer on how things should be. They might not necessarily believe in God. The teachings within the spiritual and religious genre tend to differ while other times you'll find there are some common parallels aligned with one another. The similarities are give and take by varying degrees.

One who is interested in spirituality is open to expanding their consciousness and seeking out the solutions unanswered for them. It is an individual quest to align your soul with energy bigger than the material plane. This is working on your soul and becoming a better person in the process. You want to be connected to what's beyond the current life you're living.

Sometimes one is not born spiritual, but as they evolve over the course of their life they grow to become spiritual. They might have hit rock bottom moment in life, which prompts a major transition that awakens that soul and raises their consciousness. They could have been raised in a strict religious upbringing that felt wrong to them if it was enforcing shame, guilt, and other negative feelings that are not aligned with God. To their subconscious this feels dishonest as they recall their connections while in Heaven and where they came from. They do not remember it to be a place of hate and assault. Suddenly they find themselves hip to this reality. Why do people commit horrible deeds? Why are others cruel to one another? These are some of the questions that one desires answers to that can make some measure of sense to that soul. If God exists, then how can He allow bad things to happen?

I have deep connections and communications with spirit beings that consist of guides, angels, saints, and archangels. This is no different than what anyone else can do when they elevate their consciousness, raise their vibration, and tune in to what's beyond. It is true some people are more strongly connected than others, but all souls have the capacity to elevate their consciousness, vibration, and psychic clair channels to be equally connected. Every soul connects to the Other Side whether it is believed you are in communication with your Spirit team or not. Sometimes you think that the accurate information you're coming to is your imagination or you second-guess it. Examine all of the varying belief systems that humans have designed and invented. From that point you connect the dots to where the truths within each belief system reside. There are some common denominators and similarities such as all paths lead to God. What others feel God to be is up for individual debate. The higher evolved human souls' sense that in the end it's all supposed to be about love. The further you stray from love, the more disconnected you are from spirit and God.

There are teachings that instruct you to not crave material wealth as that is a detachment from God and that the only way to true happiness is from within. While this has some measure of truth, many shun this belief just as much as they reject strict religious doctrine that insists you will go to Hell for something like French kissing. These dogmas need to be corrected and illustrated in a way that is easily digestible. The detachment from materialism needs to have the right balance, because the way Earthly life is designed today is by prospering the economy. This is the current Earthly life reality whether you agree with it or not.

Human beings need to make money to survive, to eat, to be clothed, and obtain housing. People designed it this way over the centuries of history. They implemented new ways of finding work through the rise of supply and demand. In the process, they grew detached to anything outside of themselves. You get up every morning to drive to a job to make money to be able to pay your rent or your mortgage. Most people spend the majority of their waking hours at work. This is more than at home with family, friends, and loved ones. You're taught to meet someone, get married, move in together, and start a family. These are the basics, which sound easy enough, but in the current modern-day world it's grown much more complicated than that. People have a difficult time finding a partner in crime to be with for life in a love relationship. And when they do finally find that person, it doesn't always last until the end of their days together on Earth the way it used to.

Humankind is taught how to function, and the mass majority moves along with that trend. They're taught to go to school, graduate with a High School Diploma, and start thinking of College or look for a job. They're taught to hate others who are not like them, and pass judgment, or cause harm against those who live life differently. You can be spiritually connected and still thrive to find great work that fulfills you in order to make enough to live comfortably on this planet. There are differences between becoming obsessively money hungry that you are viewed as an angry miser, to being someone who works hard, and does their job well, but you're not ruled by this job.

When you remember who you are, and you have a stronger connection of what is beyond, then the answers become clearer and God comes rushing in. Your consciousness is its own thinking, feeling, and soul inhabiting a human physical body. You are bumping into other souls inhabiting a body as well. They are also their own thinking and feeling soul inhabiting a human physical body. Why are you here? What does your consciousness remember from before your human birth? Your consciousness is the part of your soul that continues to grow wherever it moves along its life path. Your soul has been to many places. One child recalls repeated dreams of seeing both a red planet and a black one.

Another child vividly remembers Christ making him.

In essence, when any soul is born they are spiritual at heart. They are 100% in tune and psychic. They are full of immense love, joy, and peace. The soul knows where it came from. As the child grows, its environment trains them to be who it prefers it to be rather than who you really are. At that point you stray further from your soul's essence. You're having an individual spiritual journey. If you're an atheist, then that is your current spiritual journey. This is the same if you're Buddhist, Christian, Catholic, Muslim, Agnostic, and so on.

The kind of spirituality we promote is where you get to be yourself as long as it's not hurting you or anyone else. You get to be as raw, crass, and different as you like. In some spiritual circle's others have mentioned that they feel judged by someone who is on a different journey than they are. Slamming others, harassing them, and name-calling is not being spiritual or a good person for that matter. This is different than the ego rising up to resort to reacting out of anger because someone has attacked them. We're talking about those who go out of their way to attack someone for not doing something the way they might do it. This is not someone operating from their higher self. Everyone is on a different spiritual journey including a non-believer. That is their journey they've chosen to go down. As long as no one is hurting anyone, then allow that soul the freedom to explore what works for them.

Warrior of Light

There are souls living a human life that are threaded around the planet called Warrior of Light's. A Warrior of Light is a strong soul that fights in the name of Heaven, God, and the light. They are often the darker souls that ferociously defend and teach in the name of the Light. They are typically unwavering and unbending. As representatives of the Light they have no problem rising to head into battle, which they're called upon to do often even when they don't want to. Archangel Michael is the General of all Warrior of Light's. The Light is God and God is the Light. They are interchangeable energy and the all-knowing source. A Warrior of Light is someone that is a fighter or soldier for God and Heaven.

Imagine a company created by Heaven called, "The God Organization". You are one of the employees. When you need supplies, you ask God for these supplies. Sometimes He might temporarily deny the supplies due to budgetary constraints, but He is a fair boss and will provide what He believes is best for you at that time.

The Warrior of Light is not a role I'm playing, but rather it is a part of me. I do my job when I can as if I'm working for anybody else. I have off days as any human being does. The difference here is that I love this employer. When you like your employer, then it's not a drag to do the work.

CHAPTER TWELVE

Spirit Is In Your Corner

We've discussed the free will law that says no spirit being can intervene with any soul to make choices and decisions for them unless that soul has specifically requested it. This means when you desire something or you need help with anything, you send out a request to Heaven. This can be done in prayer, mentally, in writing, or out loud. If you don't ask, then they are not allowed to intervene in your life unless it is to prevent a life endangering situation that might result in death before your time. Other than that, you're on your own until you ask for help.

Your Spirit team will guide and nudge you along your path, but unless you're paying attention to these cues there is little they can do. There are some that don't believe in any of that, but the irony is they remain in a stuck and miserable position in life. If you're already stagnant and feeling hopeless, then what could it hurt to say a little quick prayer asking for help. You're already saying and thinking words and thoughts anyway, most of which are unhelpful. You may as well say a few words in prayer. No special words or invocation needs to be said. Simply saying words like this can get the ball rolling, "God can you please help me with this."

You can call upon whoever you're comfortable with communicating to such as God, Heaven, your Spirit Guide, Guardian Angel, departed loved one, Archangel, Saint, or Ascended Master. You can do this at any time or hour of the day. Whoever you are choosing to communicate to is still heard by God since there is no escape from that. Heaven understands what you desire in your heart, but they also need to hear you make the formal request. It's much like the mythological image of the Vampire, where they cannot enter your house without an expressed invitation from you. Or when a friend or employer knows you want to ask for help with something, but you're not saying anything. They wait for you to finally approach them and ask for the help you desire. This is similar in how Spirit beings in Heaven work. You need to invite them into your life if you want them working with you.

It doesn't matter how you ask, but that you do ask. You can say something like, "Please help me find another job." Or "I need help finding a love partner". You can ask them for anything. It doesn't mean that they'll always grant it, but it also cannot hurt to ask.

If you need help looking for another job, then discuss with them in prayer the kind of job you desire, but avoid laying out how you want something to come about. Leave the how and when up to them. They will orchestrate what needs to happen when the timing is right. This is pending that it is aligned with your higher self's goal. Your higher self uses the least amount of ego. While your ego might desire something, your higher self isn't interested in triviality or superficiality. You can pray to be guided to the right love partner.

Have faith and a strong belief that Spirit is in your corner, even if it feels like there is a long delay or stagnancy period going on before results appear to be forthcoming.

When I was sixteen, I knew that I was going to write books one day. I wanted to write, and no one was going to stop me in working at my passion and purpose. I knew I had to get a regular job first. I had a strong connection with my team of guides and angels when I was a child. From adolescence, I had been working with them, communicating with them, and following their guidance. I asked my team for help with getting this first job at a record store. This was back when record stores existed and were as popular as an amusement park. My team guided me in steps to make that happen.

I wanted to get into the film business not long after that, so I asked my team for help with that. I followed their guidance in trying to get in, then the lucky break took place. All great things came down from that point. It took years for something like that to happen, but it did end up happening in an even bigger way than I expected. This is an example of Heaven intervention and assistance coming through regular prayer. When I asked for help in prayer, then it eventually came to light. When I did nothing, then that was exactly what I got. I've been testing them out my entire life through trial and error. This has helped me learn the process of how they operate.

When you ask for help, guidance, or intervention, then step out of the way and allow the assistance to come about. Release and let go of the need to push for an answer or the need to control a situation. When you call up a friend you don't repeat the same phrases as if they didn't hear you the first time. You say it once and then move onto something else.

You can repeatedly request something to your Spirit team, but it will only make you grow aggravated and frustrated when you receive nothing right away. Days pass and you're feeling miserable wondering what's going on. You might say to yourself, "I don't get it. I've been praying and repeatedly asking for help with this, but nothing is coming. Maybe this isn't real or they're ignoring me."

Those in Heaven view circumstances on Earth from a different perspective than human beings. They do not get caught up in the human ego drama and tantrums that we sometimes fall into. If you feel you're being ignored, then it's likely the ego that is having a fit, which Heaven is indifferent to.

They are not fazed or affected by the ego's spectacle the way we can sometimes be.

All of the stuff in the media, human politics, and people arguing with one another is seen as triviality and a waste of time and energy from the perspective of those in Heaven. Being caught up in that space is what can cause a long delay of inactivity until you step away from being completely absorbed in pettiness.

What Heaven pays attention to is someone that has a huge growing light around them. This is someone contributing to humanity in a positive way. It is someone doing their best to be a compassionate loving person. Those are the ones that widen the eyes of a high vibrational spirit in Heaven. They want to help that soul, but sometimes they have to maneuver situations that require another person to pay attention.

For instance, you want a job at a specific company. You've put in a request for help from your Spirit team, but time has passed, and nothing has surfaced. If it doesn't come about, then take into consideration the possibilities that you're not privy to. One of them is that the person responsible for hiring staff is not paying attention to the guidance from their own Spirit team to bring you on. Another reason is that this job would not make you happy, even though you cannot see that right away. Your Spirit team can see how it would end if you joined that particular company. It would not end well in your favor, so they keep it from happening and continue to guide you to the place of employment they see you joining and being happier at. There is also the possibility that they have something greater in mind for you that is further out in the distance and you're required to have patience, faith, and trust that things are in motion behind the scenes. This concept is applied to all aspects of one's life including a desire for a loving relationship partner or a new place to move to. They might keep you away from someone you have a love crush on because they know it would not benefit your higher self. The person might be abusive in some form that would cause you prolonged heartache. When one has a love crush on someone they don't truly know that person. They've developed an ideal fantasy image over how great their crush must be while being blinded by any potential red flags. Later down the line, you connect with someone out of this world that is better than the one you had the crush on.

Putting a request into Heaven in prayer once a day can be sufficient for a desire. Put in at least one request for them on a matter before they can intervene and assist.

You're allowed the freedom to live your life the way you see fit pending it's not hurting yourself or someone else. You place your prayer request with Heaven and then you walk away. You busy yourself with other things and don't fret or think about the request you made. Let them help while you focus on something else. This is why they are called your Spirit team, because they are your team who works with you helping out where possible. You are also helping them out by taking action when they push you to. Avoid trying to think about how a prayer will be answered, because often times it's answered in a way that you do not expect.

Sometimes prayers are answered immediately and other times it may be delayed for a reason. If there are life lessons you must endure in a particular circumstance, then this could be one reason for a delay. Notice or pick up on the guidance they continue to filter through you as to why

You might find yourself saying, "I kept getting this nudge to call this person up and I continuously brushed it off. I finally called them and what I wanted came to be!"

This is an example of your Guide or Angel nudging you to make that call. Heaven communicates to you through your etheric psychic clair senses. When your senses are clear of debris, toxins, and blocks, then the clearer the messages are. This is one of the reasons they insist that everyone work on being clear minded, exercise regularly, head out into nature, take time outs, avoid negative people and choices, and watch what you ingest into your body. Those action steps contribute to you being a fine tuned up communication machine with your Spirit team. Being in nature is one of the greatest healing places to be in. The messages come in clearer in those areas.

Your Spirit team of Guides and Angels are at your disposal. Ask for help and intervention with anything you desire. Understand that there may be delays to fulfilling your request or they might have something better in mind for you. They will also only deliver what is aligned with your higher self.

Develop a daily relationship with God, Heaven, and your Guides and Angels.

They can help by giving you strength in a tough situation, motivating you to write that letter for the job you're interested in, or to obtain that potential love mate you have your eye on. If it appears that what you desire is not happening, then take into account the various possible reasons for that. When you are tuned into Spirit, then the reasons as to why will filter through you effortlessly. Centering yourself and getting your ego out of the way helps you to be more able to pick up on the possible explanations. This can be that what you're asking for is not aligned or beneficial to your higher self's growth and path. There are circumstances that need to be maneuvered in order to make it happen. Your Spirit team has a list of variables in the way that are challenging. This can be something such as working with someone's free will choice including your own.

Many human souls no longer pay attention or listen to their Spirit team's wisdom let alone believe in a higher power. Those that believe in a higher power are unaware they have a Spirit team they can connect with. They might believe the process to be associated with witchcraft or hocus-pocus. A lack of faith in your team blocks the incoming messages and guidance. Your Spirit team is relaying action steps you need to take through their guidance, but you're ignoring those steps, or brushing it off due to assuming it is wishful thinking, laziness, or procrastination. Your Spirit team will continue to give you the same guidance repeatedly until you follow it. Once you realize that the same synchronicity is continuously being put in front of you to take action on, and then you take action on it, then your Spirit team will show you the next step to take and so on as you travel along your soul's journey.

CHAPTER THIRTEEN

Be Your Own Messiah

As life on the planet continues to evolve and progress, so do many of the souls who choose to enter into an Earthly life. These souls are easy to spot since by the time they're about eight to twelve years old they have begun questioning the chaos that surrounds them. They consciously know a great deal of the madness is perpetuated by the darker sides of one's self. Discovering early on that perhaps others do not have the market cornered on the point of humanity's existence. These particularly young people are extremely sensitive and may be seen to others as different or the outcast that are hip to deception. Hence an Earth

Angel is born.

Earth Angels have a larger faith-based belief system beyond what organized religion has offered the previous generations. Organized religion has infused fear, doubt, guilt, and low self-esteem into others. These are qualities not aligned with God. The traits associated with Heaven are love, joy, and peace.

This isn't saying that organized religion has no light in it, as there is good in all groups and sects. The public only hears about the bad elements from each category of people. There are good people within the confines of organized religion that accept and love all with compassion as well too. Every soul is moving through a different class education level of spiritual growth regardless of their religious belief or non-belief. When one chooses to associate with a particular religious belief, they are moving through that level of spiritual lessons intended for that soul. Atheism is also choosing a belief system of non-belief, which is also a spiritual lesson they are moving through.

Growing up, I loved going to the church I was a part of and had no complaints about it. There was no talk of a vengeful God and nor did anyone affiliated with the church hate or disapprove of anyone that wasn't like them. I quickly and rapidly graduated beyond that as a teenager when I realized that my connections with God were happening no matter where I was. I didn't need to go to a particular place or be around a specific group of people to connect with the Other Side, because my Spirit team was moving around with me wherever I went.

When I went to Church regularly growing up, I never recalled anything negative at all associated with it from the destructive words we hear today to the negative people who claim to be Jesus followers, but are in actuality buried under the reign of the Darkness. Either I was lucky to not have heard any of that or I was just going to the right more accepting joyful churches that are based in all love. Then again I grew up during a time when there was no Internet and social media. You could be living in a bubble thinking all was well not realizing there was a great deal of condemnation and hatred going on. The public just wasn't hearing about it the way they are today.

If I ever did hear any form of hatred, lies, or damnation, I would've left immediately anyway. I don't tolerate that today and most certainly didn't tolerate it then. I have no negative memories of that at the churches I went to. I also didn't grow up in that kind of a household. I was the unusual spiritually connected one, which reveals that I had come to that conclusion on my own without any family interference or influence, but rather through my Spirit connections that have been around for as long as I can remember.

There is also quite a bit of abusive organized religious sects that condemn everyone and everything in their path. They are permanently judgmental, angry, and disrespectful lacking in compassion. Bathed in lower energies, they come from a place of fear and ego, instead of God and love. They are responsible for the massive growing number of atheists threaded throughout the planet.

Many organized religious groups have been and are so abusive, negative, and hateful that they created a vast disconnection and block with God. Instead they created a closer relationship with the darkness of ego, otherwise known to them as the Devil. They were successful in spreading false judgment out of ancient superstition that they birthed the atheist movement through this negativity. As a result, it spiritually blocked many people that grew up in that environment. You have the hate filled organized religious groups on one extreme side and then atheists on the other extreme side. Extreme sides don't bridge the gap that unites the planet together as one in compassion, unity, and love.

Someone asks their church a question about something that appears to question certain text or scripture, and no answer is given, but a generalized statement of just read the Bible and follow Christ.

This is no longer an acceptable answer to the hyper intelligent souls incarnating into an Earthly life demanding answers and solutions. Because all Earth Angels operate on a higher frequency than the norm, they're suspicious and see right through organized religions that lambast and judge others that are of a different race, gender, or sexual orientation. Naïve human adults cement this into their consciousness, as if it is true Gospel.

The Bible has beautiful passages written about showing compassion and love, but then there are texts clearly written by someone residing during a superstitious time period that no longer coincides with the awakened consciousness way of thinking. Many of my guides are from the archaic days of biblical times. Some of them made significant contributions to the Bible at that time when they were living an Earthly life, such as Luke and Matthew. Much of what they discussed in those days have been modified to one degree or another, or misinterpreted.

Mother Mary, Saint of Inner Strength

Saint Mary, Mother Mary, the mother of all Mother's often depicted with the Archangel Gabriel announcing to her of the child she would deliver to humanity. They were and are both symbols of love.

In my connections with Mother Mary, I immediately discovered what a strong ferocious soul she is. This is nothing like what is depicted in man's artwork of her which conveys a softness. She is bathed in compassion, but nowhere near being like the passivity that is portrayed of her to be. Her light and presence are immense, stable, forceful, full of overflowing love, and strength like her Son's.

My relationship with Mary dates back to childhood where I would obsessively pay homage to her image whenever I'd excitedly arrive at church as if I were going to a nightclub. A different and contradicting child, I was draped in rosary crucifixes, a filthy mouth, and a young cocky arrogance that I will do what I want, when I want, without interference.

Mary appears with this inspiring feel good inner warmth that continues to expand bigger than all the compassionate maternal beings of the world put together. The blazing sparkling rose and white light of love that shines around her outwardly like the sun is so intense that it overpowers her tiny 4'11" frame that fades into it.

The long running connection with Mary might not be surprising considering that one of my main guides Luke, who is of the Gospel of Luke, discusses Mary more than any other writer in the controversial loved and hated book. His portrait of her is layered in detail with the most quotes than any other. He's also the most educated, observant....and like myself - long winded. His stories tended to be filled with the goal of ultimate healing, which shows he had more compassion for others than some of his counterparts in the book with their superstitious fear-based dogma. When touched by Mary's power, like her Son, it is unconditional love experienced that no words can describe.

Mary urges you to be strong and persevere. When you feel like crawling into a hole, you're drained, over worked, or stressed, then call on Mother Mary to help you in healing. She coaxes you not to hide and or play the victim. You will rise up and dive straight on into battle. She believes you can do it and are stronger than you may give yourself credit for. Mary has never been passive, and she demands that you don't be either. When you draw from the Light, there is no telling what you cannot do. The Light helps you forge on even if you feel you're unable to. Let your connection with the Divine be the source of your pillar of strength.

Archangel Raphael, the Healing Angel

Archangel Raphael is known as the healing angel. This is because he has performed miraculous healing for physical, emotional, and mental issues when others have requested his help. The light that consumes him inside and out is bursting with emerald green light. Whatever he touches with this light begins the process of healing.

Call on Archangel Raphael whenever you are experiencing any issues related to physical, emotional or mental well-being. Visualize his healing green light being showered anywhere that requires attention. Understand that he may guide you to the answer that can remedy any issue. This may be from being guided to the right medical specialist or to healing medicinal properties that can assist in a medical related issue.

Raphael works alongside Mother Mary and Jesus Christ during great catastrophes where souls are extricated abruptly leaving them disoriented for a bit. The disorientation is not painful, but more of a confusing amnesia where your soul is not quite sure what's just happened.

I'm a super physically active soul and with that I've faced some physical consequences. One of them included an incident where I felt this sudden pain in my right arm or what is called the *flexor carpi radialis muscle* in the human forearm. Days passed and the pain still flushed in and out without any sign of healing. This was when I realized I needed heavenly intervention.

I called in Archangel Raphael before I went to sleep. I rubbed my hands together until I felt the heavy friction between them. I pried my hands slowly apart and clairvoyantly saw an emerald green light fire bursting between them with energy. I took that light and began hovering one of my hands over the area where the pain is. And it is done.

When I woke up in the middle of the night there were still signs of slight pain here and there, but I headed back to sleep anyway. I woke up the next day and discovered that the pain was gone. I twisted and turned my forearm and noticed no signs of any agitation or anything. Days passed into weeks and I realized that the pain had evaporated and never re-surfaced.

I believe in the power of prayer because I've witnessed and personally experienced countless and endless miracles over the course of my life as a result. When I don't ask for help, then help is not forthcoming. I've always followed and adhered to faith healing combined with medicinal healing. This is by bringing in prayer over an issue, while being guided to medicinal or herbal remedies to assist in bringing the body back to tip top form. Some only believe in faith healing, which has resulted in harm and even death, while others will pop a pill, and not bother to include Divine intervention. Their illness persists for much longer as a result, and sometimes they never get better.

Removing blockages can be done through body movement and physical exercise, which Raphael can also help with. What kind of health issues does one have that prevents them from regular exercise? For some it's...dare we say it, laziness, but for others there are some in this life that are genuinely authentically physically crippled and absolutely cannot. This applies to those who are physically capable of exercise, but just don't want to. Exercise helps in dissolving blocks with the Divine.

Archangel Gabriel, the Angel of Creative Expression

Another way to dissolve blocks is through creativity. Dive into creativity, creative pursuits, and projects when you find you're falling into a blockage. You've lost energy, passion, and a zest for life. Creative expression can assist in reopening that pathway to Divinity again. Archangel Gabriel is the one to call on to help with procrastination and in awakening your creative gifts. All Angels and Archangels are genderless and have no anatomy, despite artists depicting them in various physical forms in paintings and art. It is true they may take certain forms in appearing in ways that are recognizable to that person.

Archangel Gabriel has a feminine energy because she assists others by pulling things out from within, whether that is creative expression, passion, nurturing your inner child, mothering Children, pregnancies, or the birth of a project or endeavor. The uncertainty of how Archangel Gabriel is perceived has carried on for many centuries. This goes back to how life was lived during biblical times. Centuries ago the world was a male dominating patriarchal society, and the female form was considered forbidden and secondary. For that matter, the Catholic Church changed Archangel Gabrielle to Archangel Gabriel and demanded that she be seen, depicted, and perceived as a male. The only female deity allowed at that time was Mother Mary and that was because she gave birth to Jesus Christ.

No one can control the free will actions of mankind. This change has caused confusion over the centuries where some believe Gabriel to be male. The church eventually corrected this perception, but by that time the world was already training one another to continue to see "Gabrielle" as male.

Gabriel is an egoless genderless being unperturbed by the false beliefs of man, since all human souls have free will choice to believe what they want to believe. The "Gabriel" name may have a masculine tone to it, but gender identity is strictly reserved to human beings that have been taught and trained to separate male and female. This has also caused quite a bit issues among humankind.

Archangels and Angels will appear in a form that the individual is used to in order to be recognizable, even though it is not their natural appearance. They can morph in and out of a light source as a spirit.

It wasn't until the 1900's and beyond when women in some countries were allowed to vote or have an opinion. It was taboo for women to get a divorce or even work. Gender equality didn't really move full steam ahead until beyond the 1970's. In some countries, women are still forced to take a back seat specifically in third world countries. Therefore, it's not surprising to know that during biblical times man did not want a female deity figure.

Archangel Gabriel is my agent guiding and moving me along my career path since I started the workforce as a teenager. Luke, one of my guides, works along with her on all career work related endeavors. My writing work is done with the both of them present.

Gabriel has clairvoyantly appeared numerous times over the course of my life. Her physical appearance is neither male nor female. The shape of her face is not like a human face, but the structure of it is soft and on the feminine side, almost androgynous. She drops down into my space in a bright copper colored light with white sparkles and wears a light blue cloak that covers everything except for her face. The cloak is dominating and flowing. She also doesn't have wings even though that's how artists paint her.

When she moves into my space, I clairaudiently

hear music rush up emitting out and around her. There is a sudden intoxicating joyous uplifting feeling that soars through me. The lyrics to, "Hark the Herald Angels Sing!" were words that she whispered into the consciousness of the writers of the song. She communicates predominately through me clairaudiently and telepathically. Telepathy is one of the primary ways of communication on the Other Side.

Mother Nature's Wrath

When violence is placed upon the backs of anyone, then that can shake one's faith. There are good and bad people in all groups, except for terrorists who are against any and all that don't subscribe to their way of life. There is no room for light in that darkness. The real followers of God are peace loving people rather than fundamentalists or terrorists that scream the loudest and get the most attention from the media. They don't know God and are blinded by the infusion of Darkness. Deep down somewhere in that terrorist's soul is someone born with goodness and love inside. This concept has been brought to light in entertainment. Look at the *Star Wars* films and the character Darth Vader who was once good, but crossed over to the dark side and became evil. It wasn't until his deathbed when the goodness he once had finally came back out.

There are some that believe that Mother Nature is attempting to tell humanity something important through her majesty's destruction. They find it disheartening to see so many souls passing on as a result. This includes what some consider nature's fury and anger through Earthquakes, Fires, or Hurricanes.

From a higher level, Earthquakes and other natural disasters have to do with the construction of the Earth. God or any being in Heaven doesn't make natural disasters happen nor do they prevent them from happening. Human beings are given a place to inhabit so it's up to them to ensure it's livable. You're given a massive planet to have life on.

Like every being that exists on the planet, the planet Earth is a living-breathing organism made up of energy as every cell and atom that exists is. Energy fluctuates and compresses every second of its life reacting to the energy around it. Negative energy will aggravate all living-breathing organisms around it in a negative way since energy creates a domino effect with all that it touches.

If someone is joyful and positive, then this will uplift those around, but if they're negative and toxic, then this will bring everyone in the vicinity down. People chose to build homes on top of one another and in environments or areas that are prone to natural disasters. This isn't God's fault since He metaphorically more or less sits back and allows all souls free will to choose how they want to live life on Earth.

Nepal once experienced a bad Earthquake that caused massive devastation. Many skeptics protested to ask, "Where is this alleged, God?"

My Spirit team pointed out that those areas that were destroyed were buildings that were human-made and not up to code to withstand a catastrophic Earthquake, let alone a small Earthquake. This is all due to human decision and error, not any being in Heaven. Many people procreated at an expedited level and then inhabited areas that cannot withstand a natural disaster. The lives lost we're not lost in spiritual truth. They passed on from this plane as a collective. When catastrophes happen, it is the job of all Earthly souls to examine why and how it happened, rather than having the mindset that they're being punished.

The Archangel Michael can help with fear in any situation, but no one in Heaven can stop the Earth's plates from shifting. Earthquakes have been going on since the beginning of Earth's conception. Although some might claim that God controls natural disasters causing them to happen as punishment for some of the human sinners, which is ludicrous because the entire world sins. If he were controlling natural disasters for that reason, then He would take down the entire world in one clean swipe.

Planet Earth is an energy vessel and a ticking time bomb aggravated by the billions of energy atoms that encompass the souls that inhabit it. Regular disturbances such as hurricanes, fires, and earthquakes are not unusual, even though it's been extremely volatile. It cannot be denied that it's been shifting abnormally. God is not bringing in storms. It's the climate and nature that creates hurricanes. God doesn't care about possessions and homes. He cares about someone's character. When it is your time to go, then it's your soul contracted time.

There are also some that believe that God must love and prefer people that live in First World Countries who have access to 21st Century medicine over those that live in Third World Countries. This has been stated due to how privileged some of the rich and money hungry dominate in America primarily. God doesn't control, give, or deny anything. Tragic situations happen due to human free will choice or human incompetence. Those in First World countries are not exempt from catastrophes as they've had numerous disasters all throughout history. Some claimed that God must've hated the people of Nepal by allowing a major Earthquake to happen in 2015. The plates shifted and the Earthquake took place before anyone had a chance to pray.

It's naive to believe that God will sit there ready and able to push a button to stop a potential disaster or harm from happening simply because you want Him to. This way you can kick back, relax, and enjoy life while God sits around controlling everything to make it as pleasant and easy as possible for you. Naturally, He wants human life to be pleasant, but it's not His fault that human beings choose to govern their life through free will choice and the darkness of ego, which as a result backfires and creates harm. Who do they blame when that happens? God. He can take it regardless that it's not true. This is similar to

Children that blame what's wrong with their life on their parents. Since God is much like a parent figure and we are His children, then this metaphor is no different. Challenges are inevitable on Earth and most of the time they come about due to human free will action or through a natural disaster.

Deep Thoughts
On the Universe

The first man and woman that walked the planet spoke no words, but figured out what was needed to survive. They were guided to find food, shelter, and figured to clothe themselves. It isn't like the first person that roamed the planet stood up and tried on a suit. Clothes didn't exist and there was no shame with that. At one point, this changed where it was guessed, "Hmm, perhaps I should cover these areas."

What made him/her decide this is what should be done? If the first people that roamed the planet didn't know any better, then how would they know to do that? Where did the first man and woman come from?

Some will cite the Bible with Adam and Eve; others will cite evolution or have various other theories. No one has the market cornered, except that there had to be a first man and woman popping up from somewhere. It wasn't like, "Poof! There they are." Did they first show up as babies? Who put them there?

Those that don't believe in a higher power are unable to answer the question in a way that would make logical sense, but the extreme side has also been unable to answer it in the same logical way. This is because there is no logical understanding for the human mind to grasp how the universe came to be. This planet has grown to have nearly eight billion people on it that descended down from two people, meaning we're all descendants of what some refer to be as Adam and Eve. We are all related when you go back into time to the beginning of humankind.

The first two people on the planet we're unable to read, write, or form words in speech. Language has shifted and changed over the centuries taking on an entirely different life of its own. People set up life, dictated how it should all go, and everyone else followed.

How perfectly orchestrated it is that the planets seem to glide around the sun for billions of years in a calculated succession that has been measured in technological degrees by astrologers. A human being didn't create that orchestration. A big bang theory couldn't create a perfectly orchestrated set up with planets circling the Sun for centuries never being knocked off its axis. Besides walking on the moon, no one is up in space able to accurately detect what is going on and into the further it goes.

There is this orchestrated design of the planets swirling around the Sun never being knocked off its axis where it could hurl aimlessly through space. One of those planets contains humankind, a species that has multiplied astronomically out of control into the billions. Everything is being held together by what humans call gravity, but this is a name they gave it.

How far deep into space can you go before you hit a wall? It ends at some point and circles right back around. When you come to the awareness that this universe is dangerously deep, vast, and endless, then you realize that the noise on Earth is trivial, petty, and insignificant. None of this seemingly complex design is by accident.

Astrologers have measured how the planets seem to move in particular calculated ways around the Sun. The Universe expands and goes on for eons with numerous portals that break through into the next dimension and beyond. Where did it all come from? Who set it up that way? You can't say there is no higher power and not have a valid justifiable reason as to how this Universal design exists in its exceptional perfection. Once you believe in the higher power, then you move into where the higher power came from and what it is.

Why are eight billion people sitting on one planet alone in a Universe with no other visible life forms anywhere else? Why do those eight billion people share that space and spend it fighting, bickering, complaining, whining, posting, commenting, and attacking each other over ridiculousness? Human beings created that nonsense that has yet to lighten up. This antagonism has been going on since humankind came to be. A higher power and otherworldly figures have no time or interest for such menial trivial circumstances. They desire to see every soul raise its consciousness.

One clap in the Universe, and the Earth and everything will cease to exist. More people are growing angry in the way that others are behaving. They are welcoming something that extreme to happen to make it all go away as they've had enough. It is perplexing as to why a soul chooses to reside in the darkness of ego state around the clock. How exhausting it must be to live your life eternally in that space.

All of that and more should be the questions that every living breathing human being should be considering regardless of their personal belief systems they've chosen to follow and trust in. The answers to these questions come to life when you tune in or as you cross over back home. When that happens, you realize how superficial and trivial life was on Earth. In hindsight, you kick yourself for having been sucked into it more times than you wish you had.

It is only love that matters in the end. If parents and teachers around the world all banded together to do their job of teaching love from early on, then that would bring more love like behavior to the planet. While every bit helps, every soul on this gigantic rock needs to partake in it or the collective consciousness will be no closer to peace and love on Earth than they had ever been.

CHAPTER FOURTEEN

*The Commanding Function
of Prayer*

The power that comes with prayer is out of this world. Ask God and your Spirit team for guidance in prayer, through an affirmation, out loud, or in writing. There is no wrong way to pray. The traditional ways others have prayed are with your hands clasped together, kneeling down in a Church or by your bed. It doesn't matter how you pray, and you won't be penalized for not doing it the correct way because there is no right or wrong way. Prayer is having a conversation with God which can be done from anywhere and in any manner.

God knows what's in your heart, which means you can say one thing while attempting to shield what you truly desire. What is hidden is what God and your Spirit team already know. This is why you cannot get away with a lie in Heaven the way you can with others on Earth. They see, know, feel, and hear all. If you're doing something you know is making you guilty inside, then this guilt is a Divine nudge to honor that. At the same time, the guilt can be coming from the Darkness as well too.

The Darkness is known as the Devil in some circles, but there is a dark area in the Spirit world that runs parallel with Heaven and Earth. It is ruled by what some refer to as Lucifer, but no matter what you call it or him, the Darkness is real, and it is a place that no soul should desire to be in. I delve much deeper into this Darkness in my book, *Stay Centered Psychic Warrior*. For the purposes of bringing it up here it is to illustrate that the goal of the Darkness is to enrapture as many souls on Earth as possible. He does this because it is so extremely easy to do, as you've likely noticed if you're a psychically in tune sensitive.

One of the ways that the Darkness can get to an innocent person is by poisoning their mind with lower thoughts. It might make you feel guilty for desiring something good in your life. It will attempt to sabotage your prayers by making you think things like, "Why am I praying? This doesn't work. My prayers will never be answered."

All of the possible self-sabotaging thoughts you experience are connected to the Darkness, which doesn't want to see you or anyone else succeed.

Those that are able to wipe that away through a strong faith-based system are readily able to move back into the Light of love whenever the Darkness attempts to ensnare you.

There are endless cases over the course of history and the centuries that have passed revealing how prayer has worked and been answered in miraculous ways. One of the top steps to take when praying is to ask, but another step is to believe that your prayer is being answered. You believe it with every ounce of your entire being. This is part of what having faith is.

You are always communicating with God whether you're aware of it or not. Sitting quietly with your thoughts to anyone that will listen are prayers too. When there is trouble in your heart, then this is picked up on the Other Side. They desire to step in to help you. This can be seen when that person is troubled and feeling beaten down, but then suddenly lights up and says something that sounds like an answered prayer. They might say something like, "I just got an idea. You know what I need to do…"

Or they might get up to find an email, phone call from a friend, or be directed to something that turns everything around. Where do you think that sudden revelation came from at just the right moment? It's no coincidence that Divinely guided spirit guides and angels are actively working for God on the Other Side to help people on Earth through their often-tumultuous challenges. It would be nice if they could receive a bit more praise and acknowledgment for all of the hard work they do, but luckily for them they don't seek praise or validation the way someone on Earth might for a deed well done. They know who they are under God and have no ego filled desires that plague human beings.

I made it through the difficulties in my life through my fervent active prayer. I was praying knowing within my heart that what I needed help with would be taken care of through my faithful heart. I would eventually see what I was praying about for guidance or help with would transpire. Sometimes it was right away while the tougher long-term dreams naturally took a bit longer to maneuver. I always knew there was a reason for prayers being delayed beyond what I could see. I knew that if it was Divine will that eventually what I desired would come true. I also knew that I would need to help those prayers along by believing it would AND doing what I could through action steps. Many will pray or ask for help, but then they go back to the television set or their phones to play on them thinking that will do it. Then they later wonder why the prayer isn't getting answered. No being in Heaven is going to sprinkle blessings on a lazy or passive person that inactively waits for something to happen while mumbling complaints on it when it doesn't.

Some people pray through the act of bowing down or head down, which for some may be a sign of respect. Others may pray and look upwards because this is a position of standing in confidence allowing the power of the holy spirit to move through you. It's not because they think someone is sitting there in the sky. I've never met any faithful believer that actually believes someone is sitting in the sky on a throne. The only ones that seem to believe that delusion are atheists and non-believers. As someone with lifelong Clairvoyance and Clairaudience, spirit has always been beside me, not above or below, but next to me the way any faithful loyal friend is. The position the body makes during prayer for some is about how that person is feeling at that moment. This is the much deeper reason beyond what non-believers assume. This is also why in the past we've said that non-believers could move into believers if they moved beneath the surface of the physical and into the depths of the truth of spirit. It may seem they are incapable of great depths, but in spiritual truth they are extremely capable, but they just have to do the hard work to puncture past the physical, which takes immense mind discipline and lifestyle changes and adjustments to awaken that part of their consciousness.

I've been attacked by more atheists than hardcore religious followers. I've had atheists specifically send me condemning messages while telling their peers that it would be like clubbing a baby seal with me because of my own strong Divine belief systems that I broadcast to the world through my work. As a Warrior of Light, you are exceptionally cognizant that you when you incarnate into a human body on Earth that you are officially on the Devil's playground. He has the most control over people in this atmosphere. God wouldn't have sent you if He didn't think you could handle it.

I have always had a scientific analytical skeptical mind and I've been testing and communicating with my Spirit team since I was a child. When I say I test them, this means that I would report on when I've prayed and when I haven't. When I prayed, then what I asked for would soon come to fruition. When I did not pray, then I would notice that nothing has happened. I wouldn't continue with something if there were no results. There are more people in the world than not that believe in some form of prayer, which means that there are non-believers or people that are not religious that pray too. I've also heard from those on the fence of being a believer by folding to pray. They would say, "I've been battling this issue that I need to pray on, because I don't know what else to do."

They receive that sudden nudge from their guides that puts it in their mind to consider prayer. This nudge is coming through Claircognizance which is the psychic sense of picking up on Divine guidance through the act of knowing. You're not hearing or seeing what you need to do, but rather you just know what you need to do. Claircognizance tends to be one of the stronger psychic senses in people that are not necessarily particularly believers, but have an analytical mind. They receive light bulb moments of ideas that end up being an answer that filtered into their consciousness from the Divine.

Praying has nothing to do with religion. Anyone can pray from an atheist to a spiritual person and you are being heard. Sometimes non-believers are praying without realizing it. They've admitted to sitting quietly with their thoughts at night with the things they desire or want to see happen. Through that act they are praying. Many of them will fall down to pray when they are in a traumatic circumstance that cannot be helped by any person, but they now realize they're only hope is that there is someone out there beyond the physical plane that can help. It's usually those deeper profound moments that suddenly snap them into believers of something beyond.

Praying is also connected to the law of attraction in some ways. This is where you are believing with all your might while praying that what you desire is here now and will come to fruition. Some of the law of attraction theories have grown out of hand as we moved into the hyper social media age where anyone qualified or not can post whatever they like. Some of them master social media by amassing a plethora of followers only to feed them half-baked truths. The laws of attracting in abundance is one of those things. Because attracting in abundance and the laws of attraction are beyond just thinking positive. There is a great deal more work involved than forcing yourself to try and come off like a happy camper high on life even when you don't truly feel that way.

You ask for help in a prayer and it doesn't come to light, then you immediately believe Heaven is ignoring you or God doesn't exist. You help some of those prayers along by taking action where necessary. This is also by paying attention to your Spirit team in order to follow any instructions given. They may give you the answers you seek by communicating it through one of your psychic senses.

In some religious circles, they believe that delving into psychic practices are of the Devil. And in some atheist's circles, they believe that psychic practices are fraudulent and not real. You cannot be too extreme in anything because then it blocks you from the truth. The religious will pray on something hoping to receive an answer. They suddenly receive a positive feeling to something that tells them this is the answer. That feeling is coming through your psychic sense channel called Clairsentience, which means clear feeling. This is how the messages come through from any being that is not a physical human being. Non-believers may scoff at psychic phenomena, but the irony is they too have psychic clair sense channels built into their soul which is guiding them along their Earthly journey to make what some can call good or poor decisions depending on how they choose. The ones that are open to psychic phenomena tend to be in the middle, which is the most balanced place to be indicating they have it down.

The second you demand something in prayer will not always mean it's going to be instantly granted. The direct line to God isn't for the sake of gifts, abundance, and blessings. This is where some in the spiritual communities may receive the most criticisms. It tends to be those in that area that move to a spiritual belief system after becoming enticed by an abundance and law attracting meme. After spending years reading book after book on the law of attraction and becoming nowhere near to attracting in abundance they become skeptical and even hyper critical denouncing the entire movement of spirituality. When the truth was they were blinded by the deception of those cute memes and positive words in a book like *The Secret*. There is more to life than trying to gain as much finances as possible like it's a big lottery win. God isn't going to be helping with things like that. Soul consciousness growth work is included in the ingredients to attracting good things. He will help with some of the gifts and blessings to those that do the work.

Sometimes life lessons must be endured before those gifts and blessings are bestowed. There are other reasons for a delay with the blessings. For example, you could be asking for help in getting the big career work position you desire, but your guides are waiting for you to wrap up a toxic relationship and bring it to a close first before they guide you towards this work position desired. Sometimes there is something that has to end before something good in another area transpires. You may be perpetually guided to move to another city, and it is something you want to do, but you've been procrastinating, which delays it out for months and sometimes years. Your Spirit team is waiting for you to make this big move they've been guiding you to where what you want is waiting for you. It could be a new love interest or job that is ready for you, but not until this move is made. Perhaps the new long-term love interest is in this new city. This wouldn't be a fleeting love interest that lasts less than a year, but the love partner that lasts indefinitely.

The angels will never put you in a situation that will end up having a negative impact on you. You make choices that sometimes seem as if you were reading the signs correctly only to later discover you made an error in judgment. The more you work with them, then the easier it gets in deciphering what is indeed your Spirit team and what is not. While it's important to keep one's heart open to others, you also need to be on guard to an extent so as not to be taken advantage of.

With the angels it's about letting go of the control and allowing what is intended to fall into your lap naturally. If you feel the slightest bit of doubt or a tinge of an uncomfortable feeling within, then that would be a sign to back away from something. You would also need to pray on it and trust your Divine instincts if the doubt is the Darkness or your ego attempting to convince you that you're not deserving of good in your life. God and your Spirit team can be super subtle in Divine communication, which is why they push for you to be clear minded and to watch what you ingest as your psychic senses are highly calibrated at that moment. When your senses are calibrated, then so is the communication with them.

Let's say that your guides give you information that will come out as if it is a future prediction and then it doesn't come true. You'll begin to believe it was your imagination. If you went to a psychic reader and a prediction did not come to pass, then you would believe they were wrong and denounce all professional psychics. Psychic readers and mediums are not God, and neither is your Spirit team. They have no control over what someone does or doesn't do. They only see the projected outcome and can guide accordingly. This outcome changes from one day to the next pending on anyone's free will. While there are some psychics interested in taking advantage of a client, this is not the case with every single one. Just like any group there are both good and bad involved. The best psychics and mediums are only about 70-80% accurate on a good day. Even though like you, the soul part of themselves were born 100% psychic. Due to the heavy Earth plane with all of its toxins and blocks has dimmed that considerably. It blows right back up to 100% when you cross over back home to Heaven.

There is a job you truly want and so you ask your Spirit team for assistance in obtaining that job. If your Spirit team knows that this job is aligned with love and your higher self, then they will get to work in helping you attain this job. How they might do this is by connecting you with the person at this job who would be responsible in hiring you. If you're paying attention to the guidance of your Spirit team, then you will discover who the appropriate person is to contact at this job. You meet your Spirit team halfway by getting your resume together and forwarding it to this employer.

Your Spirit team then contacts your employers Spirit team behind the scenes through their psychic clair senses. This is in order for them to begin nudging this employer in getting that person to notice you. They may keep dropping clues in front of the employer such as getting your resume to the top of the stack. If this employer is not paying attention to the nudges and guidance that their Spirit team is putting in front of them about you, then it becomes challenging. As a result, you start to believe that your Spirit team is ignoring you and not helping you get the job. You have to keep an open mind and understand that this is not always the case.

There are several factors that come into play as to why the job offer is not happening. One of them being that this employer is not paying attention to the messages and guidance being put in front of them about you. There is a great deal of human souls who are now disconnected to anything outside of themselves, including the assistance of their own Guides and Angels. They do not have to believe in Heaven to notice the messages. Employers have pointed out that someone's name was constantly being put in front of them and they did not understand why, but it did make them take notice. They went with it and called that person anyway to offer them a job realizing it was a good move after hiring the candidate.

Your Spirit team is wrestling with someone else's free will, which people use quite bit of. Don't just ask for help, but believe that it is forthcoming and already here. If you feel abandoned by God and your Spirit team, then ask them to boost your faith. Those in Heaven would never desert the soul they're assigned to look after and guide. The reverse is that many people abandon God and head down the path guided by their ego.

It's also important to know that Heaven cannot fix everything that comes at you. You are placed in situations that you put yourself in based on past decisions. Your team will keep you away from eminent danger that could result in extreme harm or death before your time when you work with them, but they cannot ensure that everything is in working order and tip-top shape. You can drive your car all over creation every day and hope that nothing ever happens to it, but eventually something will. It will need to be serviced or the tires will need to be rotated and changed. Some of the work is up to you to take the bull by the horns and take action on.

You have a love crush on someone and want to run into them again. You ask for help and continuously run into this crush every so often. You both stare at each other with interest, but say nothing. You grow depressed thinking maybe that the crush isn't interested. You ask for Divine help in prayer again. Your Spirit team can get you both in the room together, but they cannot make you talk. That's up to the both of you to do. It's like someone can get you a job interview, but it's up to you to get the job. You're a self-sufficient thinking human being. You're not a puppet on strings that Heaven is controlling or making you walk and talk.

Your Spirit team and the object of your affections Spirit team work together to get the both of you in the room together by communicating to the both of you through your psychic senses. If you're both paying attention to your senses, then the quicker you'll have your answer on whether or not this is a positive go. If one of you isn't paying attention to their guides, then this can delay the process of bringing you together pending this is indeed the divinely guided soul mate relationship intended to happen.

Your team works with the object of your interests Spirit team to place the claircognizant idea into your mind. When this happens, then you suddenly say something like, "I need to go to the store today."

You hadn't planned to go to the store, but felt like you had to. You head off to the store only to turn the aisle and run smack into your crush.

This is also why it's important to work on raising your vibration and watching what you ingest, since a raised vibration equals clearer psychic communication with God and your Spirit team. You're able to pick up on the messages and guidance filtering into you from your team such as when to go to the store to bump into your crush.

Mark, a reader of mine in his twenties, moved into an apartment where a neighbor's cigarette smoke was blowing in the wind and into his place. He was annoyed and didn't want to close his windows since he enjoys fresh cool air breeze blowing in, but not mixed with nicotine smoke. He asked and prayed for some kind of resolve. He said, "I like this person, but I can't do the cigarette smoke."

Gradually over the course of several months he noticed the cigarette smell was gone. Eventually the neighbor ran into Mark and informed him that he quit smoking recently. He added that he was suddenly being nudged to quit. Over time the prayer helped as Mark saw the results. This is an example of a prayer being answered, but down the line. And this prayer request ended up benefitting two people. This was both the one that didn't like the smoke as well as the person doing the smoking, since it would improve the smoker's health by stopping.

Some people pray once or maybe twice, then they give up and chalk it off to not being heard. When you give up that quickly, then it's seen that you don't care about the issue being resolved all that much. You have to be fervent and consistent in your prayers.

When a catastrophic situation happens in your life, then the immediate emotional response is panic and anxiety. While in that state it lowers your vibration and cuts off the communication from Heaven. Not to mention you forget to ask for help while in that state of mind. Simply crying out with the word *help* during a state of panic can bring in heavenly assistance.

Jennifer, another reader of mine, has been in those situations where a circumstance like this has happened and she's moved into panic mode. She immediately asks for help in an alarmed state. She realizes she needs to calm down and trust that help is forthcoming. She thinks to herself during those panics, "I need to quiet my panicked mind knowing how devastating this situation is at the moment. Close my eyes and ask for help calmly."

Within the hour of the prayer, the situation is

miraculously resolved, and all is well again. She admits to feeling foolish afterwards for having panicked in the first place.

There have been numerous statistics and studies that have shown that those that pray or have a stronger faith-based system than those who do not, tend to also have a stronger well-being. Prayer has immense health benefits beyond just using prayer simply to get material things. If that's all you're praying for, then the prayers may go unanswered for some time. Prayers have immense health benefits on your soul in that it also acts like therapy being able to pray with every part of your being that it's activating those dormant dopamine cells. Prayer can ease the mind and soul when you come out of the prayer.

CHAPTER FIFTEEN

Divine Assistance

There comes a point where you've done all you can do and others are using your vessel as a sponge to absorb their drama, but won't take heed of the guidance coming in. It ends up backfiring on them when you do the opposite. They come back around, "Now what do I do?"

Well, you broke the glass on the floor, so now you need to sweep up the mess. When you move through a time of having a lack of clarity and a rise in anxiety, then this will cloud the Divine messages coming in. You're not seeing the picture clearly except what your ego wants to do.

Ask for help from your Guides and Angels. Even if you've been asking for help, you haven't seen results, and are losing faith – keep on asking and putting that energy out there. They are not ignoring you. If it is not happening right away there is a reason, but it will happen. There are obstacles and barriers being removed that are in the way to get you to that place you want to be in. Pay attention and listen for the signs that they might be giving you as well.

They may be answering and advising you, but you are not paying any attention to it as you're expecting the answer to take a different form. If you are receiving a repetitive sign that happens more than three times and benefits your higher self, then you are receiving heavenly messages. They want you to feel at peace. They want you to have enough time and resources to be able to focus and work on your life purpose. They do not want you to feel stuck at a dead-end job struggling to make ends meet for all eternity.

Communicate with God, Heaven, and your Angels daily. Pour your heart out to them in any manner you prefer, such as out loud, in prayer, in writing, in an email, or journal. Keep an eye out on any self-destructive tendencies you have a habit of doing and ask for Heavenly help with it. Taking it easy as much as possible is the best way to make it through.

I head out into nature regularly where all of the taxing physical energies are lifted off me. Partake in healthy activities that make you smile, whether that's cranking up some uplifting music, or watching a funny movie, to some lighthearted banter with a friend.

Don't give up, but keep chanting the common

phrase, "This too shall pass. This too shall pass."

Because that saying is true, since everything eventually shall indeed pass away. No circumstance lasts for all eternity. When there are testy energies swirling around you, then that's a sign to take a step back and bring in God's wall of light around you to block that out. You fall into your day to day life patterns and realize, "Wait a minute. Snap me into spiritual truth."

I've certainly had those moments where I'm struggling with something for some time, then I hear one of my spirit team members say through Clairaudience, "Do you plan on ever asking us for help on this case or are you going to continue to struggle with this on your own?"

To which I pull back, "Oh! Right. Okay."

Suddenly after asking them to help with it, it's corrected then and there by me granting permission on it.

If every single person on the planet knew or understood that there are heavenly helpers around them, then their lives would be significantly more manageable. They would view circumstances in a broader way by making sounder choices that will enhance their life even more. Having pride is by being your most authentic self and owning it.

When it comes to prayer and asking for Divine intervention and assistance, several things must be taken into account. For one, faith should be part of the equation. When doubt is included behind your words, then this can block the outcome. Include genuine gratitude for the blessings you currently have. When your prayers are all about what

Heaven can give you, then how do you think that looks? What are you contributing to help matters along?

Another factor is to pay attention to what you're psychically or intuitively picking up on from God and Spirit. What action steps are you being asked to do? Sometimes you may be asked to step outside of your comfort zone. This can create fear and anxiety prompting you to procrastinate and push off doing it. This is because you're too full of anxiety surrounding that action step. Have no fear and charge on in with what you want. This is your life and you are the owner of it. If it's another job you want, then your guides may push you to make a call, or send an email to someone that can help. When you play the game of life, then you're more apt to receiving your wishes and blessings. Ask for an increase of faith from above when you feel it waning.

Call in the Archangel Michael to extract all fear and anxiety from your aura if you're called to transform into a warrior and grab what you want without hesitation. Don't allow other people to hold you back from your dreams and desires.

Stay strong in faith knowing there is a plan. Pray and ask for help daily even if the answer isn't forthcoming right away. This isn't some blanket statement or enlightenment on a teabag, but through repetitive experience.

In an earlier chapter, I mentioned that my first job was when I was seventeen at a popular top record store chain back when those existed. Years in I was worried I was going to be there forever and would ultimately die there. Obviously that wasn't the case, but I still remember that fear feeling would plague me once in awhile. It wasn't that I hated the job. I actually did like it at the time, but it wasn't my life purpose. I had bigger dreams that I wanted to get started on. This fear feeling was a nudge telling me to not get too comfortable at that place because there is a bigger quest coming up. That's just one example out of many throughout my life. I remember feeling that stagnancy at some point fearing I'd be stuck. I prayed daily and have since I was a child. It's not just to help me with this or that. It's also to express gratitude for what I have at that time in my life that's working.

There were days that went by where I prayed, and nothing would come to light. Months would pass and still nothing. Months turned into years and suddenly out of nowhere the answer that came in was lit up like a Christmas tree and I was placed in an even better set up. There were varying time limits as to when a prayer was answered. For some instances it was immediate, while others took much longer.

If you're in a situation that you don't care for, then consider the reasons for it. Sometimes you're in a situation longer than you intended, but you're acquiring skills and traits that God needs you to collect, because it will be useful and beneficial for what's to come next. If you were thrown in what's to come too soon, then it would fail. He knows when it'll be time for the next chapter. You'll look back and then realize, "Now I know why I was at that place."

Everything I've gone through both and good bad ultimately had a benefit I gained that I was to apply to the next chapter of my life.

You work your day job to survive, but meanwhile you work on your life purpose and passion on the side. When you devote thirty to sixty minutes a day towards your purpose, then eventually that will grow over time. One day you are making enough income with that enabling you to survive doing it full time. If it's your life purpose work, then it doesn't feel like work. This is because it's your passion and it's enjoyable to dive into.

One of technologies benefits is you can watch instructional videos, seminars, read books, or listen to motivational podcasts right on your computer or phone. You can do it kicking back on the couch after a long day at work. If you're too tired after work to put any effort into your life purpose, then you can do those little action steps where you're gaining knowledge kicking back and watching, reading, or listening to motivational pieces.

Another positive beneficial reason for taking care of yourself on all levels is that it gives you more energy in the day to dive into your purpose work, even after working at another job. There are people that work more than one job. Look at your life purpose as a second job if you already have a primary job. Another benefit is that work lives are inconsistent and unstable. No one knows when the job will suddenly end and if you're able to find another job. Creating something on the side that can generate some income early on can ensure you have that extra stability should something happen.

You are sometimes thrown into situations with people that have no connection beyond anything but the superficial. It feels as if you're being tested, but there is a deeper reason for it. You have a light that is working through others even if you don't see that as it's happening or while you're in that situation with them.

I've always been super guarded and cautious over who I allow near me. I can come off aloof and cold when I truthfully have no interest in inviting in those who choose to live in harshness or meanness. I can't even force pretend that I care. I have to keep my own light protected from that darkness.

It's okay to ask for heavenly help in guiding you to an improved situation with loving people you feel more comfortable getting along with, because you deserve it. You deserve to have your prayers answered. Notice any signs or synchronicities of God's help that can sometimes come in a form you weren't expecting as well. It will keep showing up until you notice it and take action on it.

I work for God and his company we jokingly call *God, Incorporated.* Ultimately the abundance is filtered down from Him and into my life in many ways. When I need supplies, I put in a request with Him. Sometimes He grants it and other times He doesn't. I'm made aware as to if it's just a temporary delay and to be patient, or if it's because He sees that this particular supply I'm asking for will not benefit me positively in the end. My own vision may be limited to the results of what would happen if I received that particular request. Sometimes it's my own ego that desires something, not realizing I could be harmed in the end. Other times there is a temporary delay, or He plans to bring in something better that is taking a bit longer to fulfill. This also applies to you as well as anyone interested in how God works.

The enemy will always try to get in there and undo all of the work you've been doing on yourself. You cannot allow that to happen. The enemy is the darkness, the devil, the ego, or the lower self. It doesn't like progress, so it does what it can to stop you by getting into your mind and making you doubt or experience fear. You don't have to endure life alone, since that's where God comes in free of charge whenever you ask.

There is a song by Sade called "King of Sorrow", where the lyrics she sang were, "I've already paid for my future sins."

The story in the song describes someone who was working hard and not getting anywhere, but secretly longing for some kind of positive breakthrough release.

Continue to keep the faith and know that things will change one day. Sending you Divine help as you read this now and wishing you the awesome best in life, because you deserve it.

Fear Not, Because I Am With You

Who is this being of Light so great it has conjured up centuries of endless controversy and hatred in the darkness of human ego. The irony is that He is nothing that comes close to that limited view. His light has the opposite effect when you are truly standing in His presence.

Despite the toxic noise that pervades Earth by humankind, this most holy child of salvation's eminence never stops illuminating love and healing energy light off his radiance. His power and Light are so magnificent and intense that I've had to stop whatever I was doing when he's entered my vicinity because his presence is so overwhelming that it's paralyzing. Words to describe what's taking place never do it justice. It's a sense feeling of the highest most impossible love that I've never seen another human being give, but he did, and he does.

If you're down and out or experiencing any negative thought or feeling, the love of Jesus can wipe that away just by walking into your room and standing next to you. Find that space where his love resides and bathe in its vitality. The planet could learn a little something about this unconditional healing love he continuously gives without censure in a world devoid of respect.

Out of the deepest dark shines the purest light that blasts away all traces of negativity, anger, sadness, confusion, and stress from your being. If there's anything good that happens in life, it's from God. He is present for all who call on Him regardless of who you are, what you believe in, or your souls' choices this lifetime. No matter your race, gender, sexual orientation, belief or lack of belief, all are welcome to His love without judgment. You have His uncompromising permanent compassion and friendship. You are loved in ways your ego is incapable of understanding or comprehending. Those without love, those who are troubled, those wrestling with demons, you are forever loved by this being of Light free of charge. Hookers and drug users have someone who loves them unconditionally, because no one on the planet is exempt from His love.

It's less shocking to the soul that has crossed over to first see a figure they identified with on Earth. To go from a human life on Earth to human death is surprising for some. The deity they believed in or followed on Earth will appear first after death to ease them into the other plane. If you followed all deities on an equal measure, then all of them would surface. Heaven knows your consciousness and the one you would gravitate towards when it is your time to cross through the gates back home.

Why am I here? There's little that's pleasant about this place. One of the messages Jesus said was that even just a tiny bit of faith that you can spare will move mountains.

"Nothing would be impossible."

His love for you is boundless regardless if you're a believer or not. He doesn't need faith to believe in you. He already does. It already is.

What did God say?

"Fear not, because I am with you."

There's nothing you can't do when you've got your Spirit team in your house.

Affirm always: I am worthy. I deserve good. I deserve blessings. I deserve love. I deserve to be happy. I deserve peace.

CHAPTER SIXTEEN

*Scripture Reminders
on Faith and Prayer*

The purpose of this chapter is to reveal some of the more positive enlightening texts in the controversial book that can be pointed to how having an increased faith and regular prayer helps improve your life in so many ways. It doesn't matter if you're not religious or not that spiritual, but that you do believe in the power of prayer. You don't have to be religious or spiritual to partake in prayer. This is one of the great things about prayer. It's not a private club that only a select group can partake in, because anyone can partake in it including a non-believer.

In Mark 11:24 he said, "Therefore I say to you, all things for which you pray and ask, believe that you have received them, and they will be granted you."

This goes back to the mantra of ask and you shall receive, but it's more than just asking and receiving. It's also believing that you HAVE what you're asking for. This means even if you don't have it yet, you are asking as if you already have it. You can feel that you have it today. Your faith in that which you are asking for is strong enough to make it happen. God knows that you believe that He is working to help you attain your desires, pending that what you are asking for is not something that will bring about your soul's downfall. Don't worry if you think you're asking for something that will bring about pain, because He is not going to give you something like that even if you think what you're asking for will be beneficial to you. Higher beings see more than we can see at times.

In John 10:11 he said, "I am the good shepherd; the good shepherd lays down His life for the sheep."

This is more symbolism and analogy. Jesus is the shepherd that watches over the sheep. A good shepherd is devoted to the sheep and will die for them. That's how loyal and devoted he is. In this case, Jesus is the shepherd and the sheep are everyone that puts their trust in him. When you put your faith and trust in him, then he will not disappoint, because he values loyalty. This isn't to be confused with a master servant situation or that he has an ego and demands this love. This is more about being a devoted loyal person that has a tight relationship with God. This carries over to all aspects of your life if this is your overall character. People will disappoint you and betray your trust, but God's devotion is constant.

When a good person knows that someone loves them, then they will do whatever they can to appease that person. When employees at a job know they are taken care of and adored by their employer, then those employees tend to work harder with a happier disposition because somewhere in the employee's soul they can feel the goodness that comes with respect and loyalty. This same concept can be transferred to prayer and your relationship with God knowing that you have someone that loves and adores you and wants to see you thrive, but also wants to see you put some fight into your life too.

In Luke 6:45 he said, "Good people do good things because of the good in their hearts, but bad people do bad things because of the evil in their hearts. Your words show what is in your heart."

This can be applied to critical complaining. The complainer is showing what's in their heart through these complaints. Witness all those rants on social media. Each of those posters reveal what is truly going on inside them. You may ask for something and believe you're good, but if you're complaining then you are showing yourself to be a critical soul which doesn't bring in anything good.

If you are out in the world doing what you can to help others in some positive way, and you are praying for blessings, then these good acts you've been doing count in the doing good equation. Those prayers tend to get answered quicker over the lazy passive soul's prayers that pray once or twice, then they go to crack open another beer and sit on the couch day after day waiting for the doorbell to ring with that good news. God wants to see you get up and put some fight in your life!

In Luke 11:9 he said, "So I say to you, ask, and it will be given to you; seek, and you will find; knock, and it will be opened to you."

This means you ask in prayer for your request and it is done, but the scripture goes further, seek and you will find. Sometimes what you're looking for is right in front of you. When you take it a step further beyond just asking for something and begin seeking it out on your own as well to help it along, then this shows God and your Spirit team how serious you are about receiving this blessing you are asking for.

Knock and it will be opened to you. When you knock on a door, you are knocking more than once, but a few times until someone finally opens it. You are being requested to ask in prayer for what you want, but also seek what you desire through action. This is showing God what you're willing to do to get what you want. Notice the feeling of a door opening wide to what you've been asking for and how that will make you feel.

In John 14:27 he said, "Let not your heart be trouble neither let it be afraid."

In Mark 5:36 he said something similar, "Be not afraid, only believe."

And in Luke 12:32 he said, "Fear not, little flock; for it is your Father's good pleasure to give you the Kingdom."

All of those scriptures point to boosting your faith and knowing that all things are possible through faith. You might be feeling fear, doubt, or anxiety about something good never happening for you, but those scriptures point to you experiencing those traits as being a candidate for blessings.

In Matthew 9:22 he said, "Be of good comfort; your faith has made you whole."

This is saying that by increasing your faith and believing that through God and spirit all things are possible. This is because it is this boosted faith, which fills you from within that gives you the courage to rise up into warrior of light mode knowing that you are being guided purposively. There is nothing that you cannot do, accomplish, and gain through faith.

Matthew also said this again in 19:26, "With God all things are possible."

In Luke 6:38 he said, "Give, and it shall be given unto you."

This is hammering home the idea that it isn't always about praying to get prayers answered. What are you giving to the world to positively better humanity and others?

Humanitarians have quite a number of Guides and Angels that have entered their life to work with them. When the humanitarian has those frequent moments of wanting to throw in the towel or they doubt God, then that persons Spirit team lifts their heart and mind in order to motivate the soul to continue on. Sometimes they do this by infusing a sudden burst of energy that is an uplifting motivating feeling within you. This is after hearing your prayer or cry out for help.

For some, you agreed to an Earthly life for a specific purpose geared toward the world at large. When you falter on your path, then your Spirit team coaxes you onward. This is also why your soul's purpose can never truly go away, because it is innate in your soul's DNA. It's part of your contract, which you have access to in the deepest regions of your psychic mind. One of the roles of your Spirit team is to make sure you fulfill elements of your soul's contract. Your purpose is part of the giving in the giving and receiving equation. When you give then you will receive.

In Luke 6:37 he said, "Forgive, and you shall be forgiven."

If you have any pain in your heart, then through prayer ask for forgiveness if you feel you've done something to warrant that guilt. You don't need to drone on about it falling to your knees in dramatic ways. Simply stating that you'd like help with them lifting the heavy burdens of guilt from your heart will work in your favor.

In Matthew 26:41 he said, "Watch and pray, that you enter not into temptation."

This also has to do with praying and asking for blessings, but then you go off and partake in activities that you know are harmful to your soul. If you pray, then you go over to social media to attack people and complain, then you've missed the point of prayer. You're not doing the work and walking the talk of having complete spiritual faith.

In Matthew 7:7 he said, "Seek, and you shall find."

This has been said numerous times throughout the holy book and takes on endless meanings. In this case it's about delving deep to reach those Divinely guided answers. It's you venturing on that soul spiritual quest to uncover truths that can help expand your soul and propel you further into enlightenment.

In Matthew 5:14 he said, "You are the light of the world."

Don't forget you have agreed to an Earthly life to shine that light of your soul onto the world through the compassionate acts and deeds you put forth in your life. This can also be by being your highest best self whenever and wherever possible. You are helping someone out there even if you're telling your story. You are motivating, inspiring, and encouraging someone else. You are treating others with kindness and compassion, while steering clear of those that have hate in their hearts.

Last but certainly not least in Luke 21:36 he said, "Pray always."

I don't think you can get any clearer than that. Make prayer part of your daily life. Don't just pray whenever you need something. Pray to develop a stronger relationship with God and your Spirit team. Prayer is like vitamins that you have to take daily before you begin to see positive results within and around you. It's not for the sake of blessings, but to completely transform and evolve your soul consciousness in being one with the Light. You were part of this Light upon your soul's conception, but might have lost your way in the dark regions of Earthly life.

You may ask for certain material blessings, but how long will those physical materials last? When you pass on from this life, then those material items will become obsolete and meaningless, but where will your soul be? You spent your life demanding you receive material items in prayer, but where's your heart and your soul in all this?

It's okay to ask for material necessities such as things that can help you survive such as a steady income, a place to live, food, clothes, etc. Those are necessities a human being needs to survive on this plane. God understands that, but it's more than just asking for material abundance. It's also asking to be awakened to the light and diving deeper beneath all of the physical longings. The material that comes into the faithful warrior heart is a positive side effect to evolving your soul consciousness.

Pray always, pray daily, pray with passion, pray with intent, pray with action, pray with faith. Prayer is one of the most powerful spiritual things you can do to improve you, your soul, those around you, circumstances, and your life one day at a time.

Acknowledgments

Thank you to God, my Spirit Team Council, and to all of the loyal readers that have hopped on this awesome train ride of mine and stayed on. I am forever blessed and grateful for your eternal support of the work we do. Thank you also for supporting the arts and the artists of the world.

ALSO BY KEVIN HUNTER

Stay Centered Psychic Warrior
Warrior of Light
Empowering Spirit Wisdom
Darkness of Ego
Realm of the Wise One
Transcending Utopia
Reaching for the Warrior Within
Spirit Guides and Angels
Soul Mates and Twin Flames
Raising Your Vibration
Divine Messages for Humanity
Connecting with the Archangels
Monsters and Angels
The Seven Deadly Sins
Love Party of One
Twin Flame Soul Connections
A Beginner's Guide to the Four Psychic Clair Senses
Tarot Card Meanings
Attracting in Abundance
Abundance Enlightenment
Living for the Weekend
Ignite Your Inner Life Force
Awaken Your Creative Spirit
The Essential Kevin Hunter Collection
Metaphysical Divine Wisdom (Series)

STAY CENTERED PSYCHIC WARRIOR

*A Psychic Medium's Trip Through the Darkness and Light of the
Spirit Worlds, and Other Paranormal Phenomena*

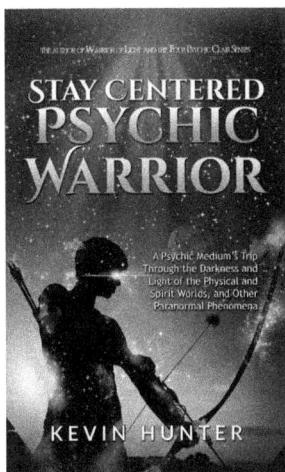

In *Stay Centered Psychic Warrior*, metaphysical teacher, psychic, medium, and author, Kevin Hunter talks about what it's like battling between mental health issues and the deeply potent psychic input that continuously falls into his soul's consciousness throughout each day. He offers plenty of examples and discussions of his brushes with spirit, seeing and hearing the dead, the power of the Darkness and the Light in both the physical and spirit worlds, along with sharing his numerous personal psychic and mediumship essays, glimpses of the Other Side, near death experiences, past lives, soul contracts, traveling to and from the Spirit Worlds, spirit guides and angels, recognizing your own psychic gifts, and much more!

This unique autobiography focuses on psychic and mediumship related content coupled with the soul's journey and purpose. Stay Centered Psychic Warrior is an intensely forceful and revealing read that doesn't shy away from the uncomfortable, the Darkness, abuse, mental health issues, while uplifting it with the many blessings of the Light and intriguing day to day psychic phenomena all in one. Allow it to inspire you to recognize your own psychic gifts knowing there is much more to this Earthly life than can be seen or comprehended. Be empowered to break through the rubble and stand strong and centered under the powerful Light that shines through any Darkness.

A Beginner's Guide to the
FOUR PSYCHIC CLAIR SENSES

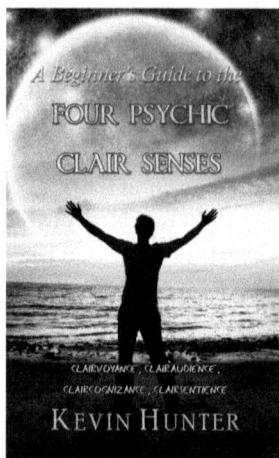

Many believe psychic gifts are bestowed upon select chosen ones, while others don't believe in the craft at all. The reality is every soul is born with heightened psychic gifts and capabilities, but somewhere along the way those senses have dimmed. All are capable of being a conduit with the Other Side, including those closed off and blocked to it. There are a variety of enlightened beings residing in the spirit realms to assist human souls that request their help. They use varying means and methods to communicate with you called clair channels. These clairs are crystal clear etheric senses used to communicate with any higher being, spirit guide, angel, departed loved one, archangel, and God.

The *Four Psychic Clair Senses* illustrates what the core senses are, examples of how the author picks up on messages, how you can recognize the guidance, and other fun metaphysical psychic stuff. You are a walking divination tool that allows you to communicate with Spirit. The clairs enable you to receive heavenly messages, guidance, and information that positively assist you or another along your Earthly journey. Read about the four core clairs in order to pinpoint what best describes you and how to have a better understanding of what they are and how they work for you.

TAROT CARD MEANINGS

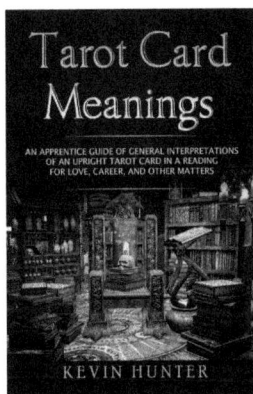

Tarot Card Meanings is an encyclopedia reference guide that takes the Tarot apprentice reader through each of the 78 Tarot Cards offering the potential general meanings and interpretations that could be applied when conducting a reading. The meanings included can be applied to most anything whether it be spiritual, love, general, or work-related questions.

Many novices struggle with reading the Tarot as they want to know what a card can mean in their readings. They grow stuck staring at three cards side by side and having no idea what it could be telling them. The Tarot Card Meanings book can assist by pointing you in the general direction of where to look. It will not give you the ultimate answers and should not be taken verbatim, as that is up to you as the reader to come to that conclusion. The more you practice, read, and study the Tarot, then the better you become.

Tarot Card Meanings avoids diving into the Tarot history, or card spreads and symbolism, but instead focuses solely on the potential meaning of a card in a general, love, or work reading. This gives you a structure to jump off of, but it is up to you to take that energy and add the additional layers to your reading, while trusting your higher self, intuition, instincts and Spirit team's guidance and messages. Anything included in the Tarot Card Meanings book is an overview and not intended to be gospel. It is merely one suggested version of the potential meanings of each of the 78 Tarot cards in a reading. It may assist the novice that is having trouble interpreting cards for themselves.

ALSO AVAILABLE BY KEVIN HUNTER

Books that Empower, Enlighten, Educate, and Entertain!

*Just as your body needs physical food to survive,
your soul needs spiritual food for well-being nourishment.*

THE ESSENTIAL KEVIN HUNTER COLLECTION

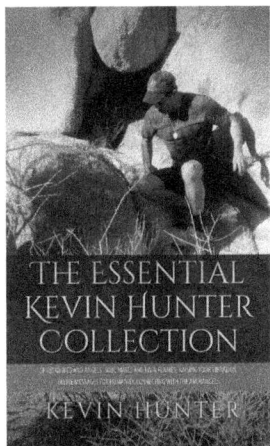

Kevin Hunter an empowering author specializing in a variety of genres, but he is most notably known for his work in the realms of spirituality, metaphysical, and self-help. He has assisted people around the world with standing in their power, and in having a stronger connection with Heaven, while navigating the materialistic practical world. Now some of his popular spiritually based books are available in this one gigantic volume.

The Essential Kevin Hunter Collection is the spiritual bible that contains over 500 pages of content geared towards improving and enhancing your life. It is for those who prefer to have everything in one gigantic book. The content included in this edition are from the books: *Spirit Guides and Angels, Soul Mates and Twin Flames, Raising Your Vibration, Divine Messages for Humanity, Connecting with the Archangels, Warrior of Light, Empowering Spirit Wisdom, and Darkness of Ego.*

TRANSCENDING UTOPIA
Reopening the Pathway to Divinity

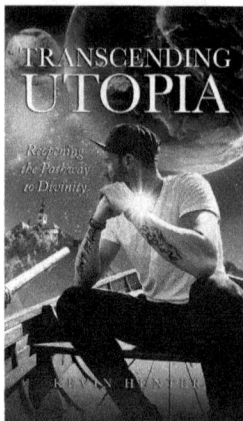

Transcending Utopia is packed with practical and spirit knowledge that focuses on enhancing your life through empowering divinely guided spiritual related teachings, inspiration, wisdom, guidance, and messages. The way to accelerate existence on Earth towards Utopia is if every person on the planet resided in their soul's true nature, which is in a state of all love, joy, and peace. The ultimate Nirvana is surpassing that perfection through methods that a limited consciousness could ever dream possible. This is the exceptional glory your soul was born into before the dense turbulence of Earthly life enveloped and suffocated you.

Transcending Utopia is to go beyond your limits and travel outside of the generic mundane materialistic achievement that human beings taught one another to thrive for. A utopian society is where everything is perfectly blissful on all levels according to the sanctified values you were born with. The sensations connected to how flawless everything feels in that moment reveals the authentic perfection you were made from. Utopia is the ideal paradise as imagined in one's dreams that seems to be inaccessible by human standards. It is a state of mind that is possible to reach by adopting broader ways of looking at circumstances while being disciplined about how you conduct your life. You search for a sign of this utopia through external means, only to be consistently left with disappointment. This is because utopia begins and ends inside the spark that burns within your spirit like a pilot light waiting to be ignited.

LIVING FOR THE WEEKEND
The Winding Road Towards Balancing
Career Work and Spiritual Life

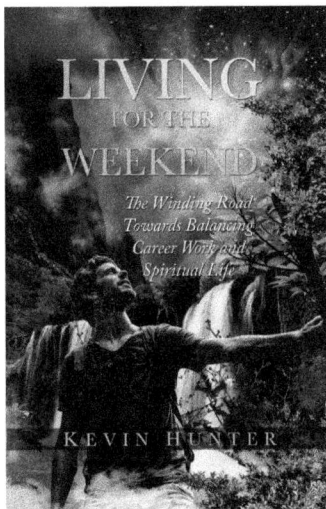

Working hard to ensure your bills are paid can leave your soul spiritually starved for soul nourishment. When your ultimate goal is to obtain enough money to be comfortable that you become carried away in that current, then there is little to no room for Divine enrichment.

Many work to survive in jobs they hate because it's the way it is. As a result, they experience and endure all sorts of emotional pain whether it is through depression, sadness, anger, or any other kind of negative stressor. Some silently suffer through this emotional strain gradually killing off their life force. If you don't have a healthy social life and positive fun filled activities and hobbies to balance that burden outside of that, then that could add additional tension. What's it all for if you can't live the life you've always wanted to live? Instead, you spend your days growing forever miserable and broken.

Living for the Weekend examines the pitfalls, struggles, as well as the benefits available in the current modern-day working world. This is followed up with spiritual and practical tips, guidance, messages, and discussions on ways to incorporate more balance and enlightenment to a cutthroat material driven world.

Attracting in Abundance
*Opening the Divine Gates to Inviting in Blessings and Prosperity
Through Body, Mind, and Soul Spirit*

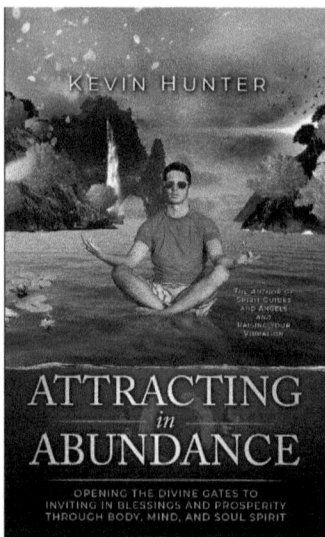

Having enough money to survive comfortably enough on this physical plane is part of obtaining abundance, but it's not the destination and purpose to thrive for. You could work hard to make enough money to the point you are set for life, but that won't necessarily equate to happiness. Achieving a content satisfied state of joy and serenity starts with examining your soul's state and overall well-being. When that's in place, then the rest will follow.

Attracting in Abundance combines practical and spirit wisdom surrounding the nature of abundance. This is something that most everyone can get on board with because all human beings desire physical comforts, blessings, and prosperity, regardless of their personal values and belief systems. *Attracting in Abundance* is broken up into three parts to help move you towards inviting abundance into your life on all levels. "Part One" contains some no-nonsense lectures surrounding the philosophies, concepts, and debates on the laws of attracting in abundance. "Part Two" is the largest of the sections geared towards fine tuning the soul into preparing for abundance. "Part Three" is the final lesson plan to help crack open the gates of abundance with various helpful tidbits, guidance, and messages as well as the blocks that can prevent abundance from coming in.

The B-Side to the Attracting in Abundance book

ABUNDANCE ENLIGHTENMENT
An Easy Motivational Guide to
the Laws of Attracting in Abundance
and Transforming Your Soul

Ultimate authentic success surrounds your soul's growth and evolving process. It's when you realize that none of the physical ego driven desires matter in the end. You can work hard to make sure you stay afloat, you're able to pay your bills, and support yourself and family, but you're not chasing popularity for external validation. Any amount of goodness displayed from your heart is the true measure of real accomplishment.

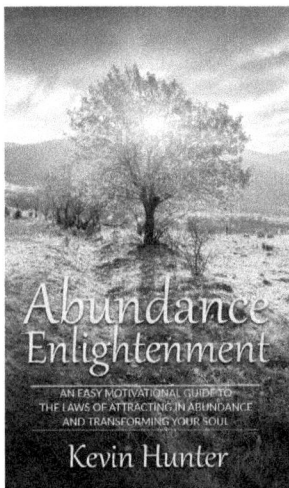

An overflowing feeling of optimism and love coupled with faith and action is what increases the chances of attracting good things and positive experiences to you. Abundance is more than monetary and financial increase. It can also be about reaching an optimistic well-being state of joy, peace, and love. This positive emotional mindful state simultaneously attracts in blessings.

Abundance Enlightenment is the follow up book to *Attracting in Abundance*. It contains both practical guidance and spirit wisdom that can be applied to everyday life. Some of the key topics surround the laws of attraction as well as healthier money management and improving your soul to help make you a fine tuned in abundance attractor.

MONSTERS AND ANGELS
An Empath's Guide to Finding Peace in a Technologically Driven World Ripe with Toxic Monsters and Energy Draining Vampires

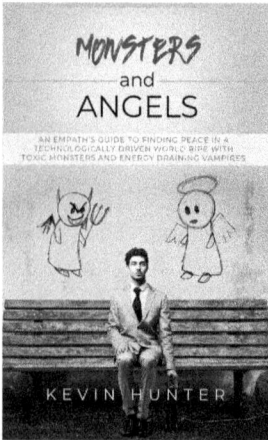

Every person on the planet is capable of being empathic and sensitive, to becoming an energy vampire or toxic monster. No one is exempt from displaying the darker sides of their ego. The easiest and most efficient way to spread any kind of energy is online. Every time you log onto the Internet, there is a larger chance you're going to see something related to the news, media, or gossip areas thrown in front of you, even if you attempt to avoid it as much as possible. You're absorbing everything that your consciousness faces, including the ugly and the wicked, which has its own consequences. This tempestuous energy is tossed into the Universe ultimately creating a flame-throwing battleground inside and around you.

Monsters and Angels discusses how technology, media, and social media have an immense power in distributing both positive and negative influences far and wide. This is about being mindful of what can negatively affect your state of being, and how to counter and avoid that when and wherever possible. This is why it's beneficial to govern yourself, your life, and your surroundings like a strict disciplined executive.

TWIN FLAME SOUL CONNECTIONS
Recognizing the Split Apart, the Truths and Myths of Twin Flames,
Soul Love Connections, Soul Mates, and Karmic Relationships

Twin Flames have a shared ongoing sentiment and quest from the moment they're a spark shooting out of God's love that explodes into a blinding white fire that breaks apart causing one to be two, until two become one again, separate and whole, and back around again. Looking into the eyes of your Twin Flame is like looking into the eyes of God, because to know love is to know God.

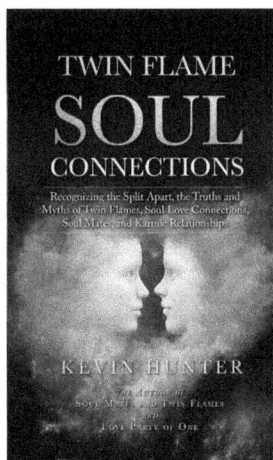

TWIN FLAME SOUL CONNECTIONS
Recognizing the Split Apart, the Truths and Myths of Twin Flames, Soul Love Connections, Soul Mates, and Karmic Relationships

KEVIN HUNTER

Twin Flame Soul Connections discusses and lists some of the various myths and truths surrounding the Twin Flames, and how to identify if you've come into contact with your Twin Flame, or if you know someone who has. The ultimate goal is not to find ones Twin Flame, but to awaken one's heart to love, and to work on becoming complete and whole as an individual soul through spiritual self-mastery, life lessons, growth, and raising your consciousness. Your soul's life was born out of love and will die right back into that love.

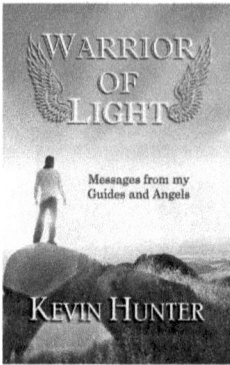

WARRIOR OF LIGHT
Messages from my Guides and Angels

There are legions of angels, spirit guides, and departed loved ones in heaven that watch and guide you on your journey here on Earth. They are around to make your life easier and less stressful. Learn how you can recognize the guidance of your own Spirit team of guides and angels around you. Author, Kevin Hunter, relays heavenly guided messages about getting humanity, the world, and yourself into shape. He delivers the guidance passed onto him by his own Spirit team on how to fine tune your body, soul and raise your vibration. Doing this can help you gain hope and faith in your own life in order to start attracting in more abundance.

EMPOWERING SPIRIT WISDOM
A Warrior of Light's Guide on Love, Career and the Spirit World

Kevin Hunter relays heavenly, guided messages for everyday life concerns with his book, *Empowering Spirit Wisdom*. Some of the topics covered are your soul, spirit and the power of the light, laws of attraction, finding meaningful work, transforming your professional and personal life, navigating through the various stages of dating and love relationships, as well as other practical affirmations and messages from the Archangels. Kevin Hunter passes on the sensible wisdom given to him by his own Spirit team in this inspirational book.

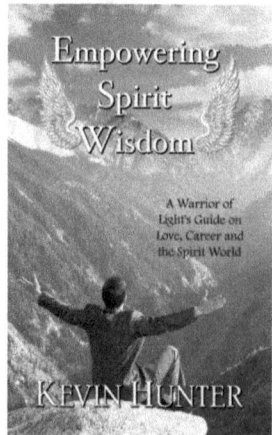

DARKNESS OF EGO

In *Darkness of Ego*, author Kevin Hunter infuses some of the guidance, messages, and wisdom he's received from his Spirit team surrounding all things ego related. The ego is one of the most damaging culprits in human life. Therefore, it is essential to understand the nature of the beast in order to navigate gracefully out of it when it spins out of control. Some of the topics covered in *Darkness of Ego* are humanity's destruction, mass hysteria, karmic debt, and the power of the mind, heaven's gate, the ego's war on love and relationships, and much more.

REACHING FOR THE WARRIOR WITHIN

Reaching for the Warrior Within is the author's personal story recounting a volatile childhood. This led him to a path of addictions, anxiety and overindulgence in alcohol, drugs, cigarettes and destructive relationships. As a survival mechanism, he split into many different "selves". He credits turning his life around, not by therapy, but by simultaneously paying attention to the messages he has been receiving from his Spirit team in Heaven since birth.

REALM OF THE WISE ONE

In the Spirit Worlds and the dimensions that exist, reside numerous kingdoms that house a plethora of Spirits that inhabit various forms. One of these tribes is called the Wise Ones, a darker breed in the spirit realm who often chooses to incarnate into a human body one lifetime after another for important purposes.

The *Realm of the Wise One* takes you on a magical journey to the spirit world where the Wise Ones dwell. This is followed with in-depth and detailed information on how to recognize a human soul who has incarnated from the Wise One Realm. Author, Kevin Hunter, is a Wise One who uses the knowledge passed onto him by his Spirit team of Guides and Angels to relay the wisdom surrounding all things Wise One. He discusses the traits, purposes, gifts, roles, and personalities among other things that make up someone who is a Wise One. Wise Ones have come in the guises of teachers, shaman, leaders, hunters, mediums, entertainers and others. *Realm of the Wise One* is an informational guide devoted to the tribe of the Wise Ones, both in human form and on the other side.

IGNITE YOUR INNER LIFE FORCE

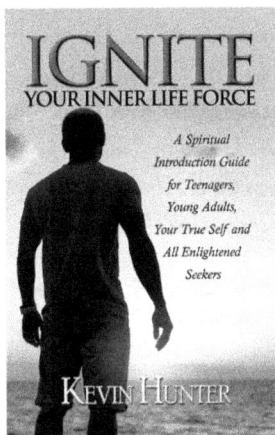

Ignite Your Inner Life Force is an introduction guide for teens, young adults, and anyone seeking answers, messages, and guidance and surrounding spiritual empowerment. This is from understanding what Heaven, the soul, and spiritual beings are to knowing when you are connecting with your Spirit team of Guides and Angels. Some of the topics covered are communicating with Heaven, working with your Spirit team, what your higher self is, your life purpose and soul contract, what the ego is, love and relationships, your vibration energy, shifting your consciousness and thinking for yourself even when you stand alone. This is an in-depth primer manual offering you foundation as you find a higher purpose navigating through your personal journey in today's modern-day practical world.

AWAKEN YOUR CREATIVE SPIRIT

Your creative spirit is more than being artistic and getting involved in creativity pursuits, although this is a good part of it. When your creative spirit is activated by a high vibration state of being, then this is the space you create from. You can apply this to your dealings in life, your creative and artistic pursuits, and to having a greater communication line with your Spirit team on the Other Side. *Awaken Your Creative Spirit* is an overview of what it means to have access to Divine assistance and how that plays a part in arousing the muse within you in order to bring your state of mind into a happier space.

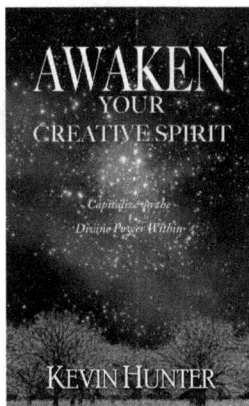

THE *WARRIOR OF LIGHT* SERIES OF POCKET BOOKS

*Spirit Guides and Angels, Soul Mates and Twin Flames,
Raising Your Vibration, Connecting with the Archangels,
Twin Flame Soul Connections, Attracting in Abundance,
Monsters and Angels, The Four Psychic Clair Senses, The
Seven Deadly Sins, Love Party of One, Abundance
Enlightenment,* and *Divine Messages for Humanity*

METAPHYSICAL DIVINE WISDOM
BOOK SERIES

On Psychic Spirit Team Heaven Communication
On Soul Consciousness and Purpose
On Increasing Prayer with Faith for an Abundant Life
On Balancing the Mind, Body, and Soul
On Manifesting Fearless Assertive Confidence
On Universal, Physical, Spiritual and Soul Love

♥

About Kevin Hunter

Kevin Hunter is the metaphysical author of dozens of spiritually based books that include *Warrior of Light, Transcending Utopia, Stay Centered Psychic Warrior, Metaphysical Divine Wisdom Series, Empowering Spirit Wisdom, Realm of the Wise One, Reaching for the Warrior Within, Darkness of Ego, Living for the Weekend, Ignite Your Inner Life Force, Awaken Your Creative Spirit,* and *Tarot Card Meanings.*

His pocketbooks include, *Spirit Guides and Angels, Soul Mates and Twin Flames, Raising Your Vibration, Divine Messages for Humanity, Connecting with the Archangels, The Seven Deadly Sins, Four Psychic Clair Senses, Monsters and Angels, Twin Flame Soul Connections, Attracting in Abundance, Love Party of One* and *Abundance Enlightenment.* His non-spiritual related works include the horror drama, *Paint the Silence,* and the modern-day love story, *Jagger's Revolution.*

Kevin started out in the entertainment business in 1996 as the personal development assistant guy to one of Hollywood's most respected acting talents, Michelle Pfeiffer, at her former boutique production company, Via Rosa Productions. She dissolved her company after several years and he made a move into coordinating film productions for the studios. His film credits include *One Fine Day, A Thousand Acres, The Deep End of the Ocean, Crazy in Alabama, The Perfect Storm, Original Sin, Harry Potter & the Sorcerer's Stone, Dr. Dolittle 2,* and *Carolina.* He considers himself a beach bum born and raised in Southern California. For more information and books visit: www.kevin-hunter.com